The Book
of Embraces

Also by Eduardo Galeano

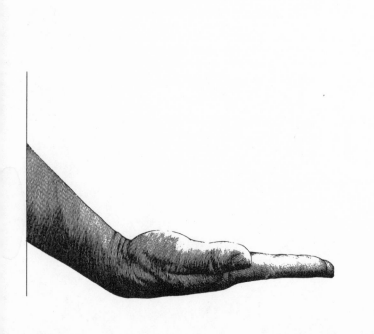

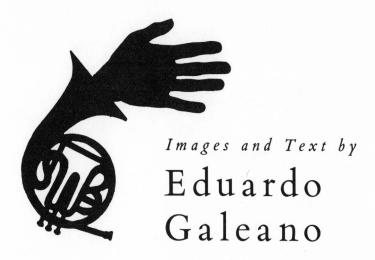

Images and Text by
Eduardo Galeano

*Translated by
Cedric Belfrage
with Mark Schafer*

The Book
of Embraces

W·W·Norton & Company

NEW YORK   LONDON

The text of this book is composed in 12/13 Bembo,
with the display set in Bembo.
Composition and manufacturing by the Haddon Craftsmen, Inc.
Book design by Eduardo Galeano and Margaret Wagner.

First Edition.

Library of Congress Cataloging-in-Publication Data
Galeano, Eduardo H., 1940–
[Libro de los abrazos. English]
The book of embraces / by Eduardo Galeano ; translated by Cedric
Belfrage with Mark Schafer.
p.   cm.
Translation of: El libro de los abrazos.
I. Title.
PQ8520.17.A4L513   1991
863—dc20   90–21337

ISBN 0–393–02960–3

W.W. Norton & Company, Inc.
500 Fifth Avenue, New York, N.Y. 10110
W.W Norton & Company, Ltd.
10 Coptic Street, London WC1A 1PU

1 2 3 4 5 6 7 8 9 0

TRANSLATOR'S ACKNOWLEDGMENT

Within days of embarking on this noble project, a series of disabling traumas threatened its completion, which was then made possible by my friend and neighbor, the young translator Mark Schafer. For so generously sharing his skills and patience, I owe him eternal thanks.

C.B.
Cuernavaca, Mexico

Cedric Belfrage murió poco después
de terminar la traducción de este libro.
Hacía ya muchos años que trabajábamos
juntos. Cada una de sus traducciones
aumentaba nuestra certeza de mutua
identificación. Yo me reconocía en sus
versiones y él se sentía traicionado y
se enojaba cuando yo no escribía lo
que él hubiera escrito.

> Una parte de mí murió con él.
> Una parte de él vive conmigo.

Cedric Belfrage died shortly after
finishing his translation of my work
The Book of Embraces. We had already
worked together for many years. Each one
of his translations increased our certitude
of mutual identification. I would recognize
myself in each of his translations and
he would feel betrayed and annoyed
whenever I didn't write something the
way he would have.

> A part of me died with him.
> A part of him lives with me.

EDUARDO GALEANO

*R*ecordar: To remember; from the Latin *re-cordis*,
to pass back through the heart.

The Book
of Embraces

This book is dedicated
to Claribel and Bud,
to Pilar and Antonio,
to Martha and Eriquinho

THE WORLD

A man from the town of Neguá, on the coast of Colombia, could climb into the sky.

On his return, he described his trip. He told how he had contemplated human life from on high. He said we are a sea of tiny flames.

"The world," he revealed, *"is a heap of people, a sea of tiny flames."*

Each person shines with his or her own light. No two flames are alike. There are big flames and little flames, flames of every color. Some people's flames are so still they don't even flicker in the wind, while others have wild flames that fill the air with sparks. Some foolish flames neither burn nor shed light, but others blaze with life so fiercely that you can't look at them without blinking and if you approach, you shine in fire.

THE ORIGIN OF THE WORLD

The Spanish war had ended only a few years back, and the Cross and the Sword reigned over the ruins of the republic. One of the defeated, an anarchist worker fresh out of jail, was looking for a job. He scoured heaven and earth in vain. There was no work for a Red. Everyone looked daggers at him, shrugged their shoulders and turned their backs. No one would give him a chance, no one listened to him. Wine was the only friend he had left. At night, before the empty dishes, he bore in silence the reproaches of his saintly wife, a woman who never missed Mass, while his son, a small boy, recited the catechism to him.

Some time later, Josep Verdura, the son of this accursed worker, told me the story. He told me in Barcelona, when I arrived there in exile. He had been a desperate child who wanted to save his father from eternal damnation, and the ever atheistic and stubborn fellow wouldn't listen to reason.

"But papá," Josep said to him, weeping. *"If God doesn't exist, who made the world?"*

"Dummy," said the worker, lowering his head as if to impart a secret. *"Dummy. We made the world, we bricklayers."*

Diego had never seen the sea. His father, Santiago Kovadloff, took him to discover it.

They went south.

The ocean lay beyond high sand dunes, waiting.

When the child and his father finally reached the dunes after much walking, the ocean exploded before their eyes.

And so immense was the sea and its sparkle that the child was struck dumb by the beauty of it.

And when he finally managed to speak, trembling, stuttering, he asked his father:

"Help me to see!"

GRAPES AND WINE

On his deathbed, a man of the vineyards spoke into Marcela's ear. Before dying, he revealed his secret:

"The grape," he whispered, *"is made of wine."*

Marcela Pérez-Silva told me this, and I thought: If the grape is made of wine, then perhaps we are the words that tell who we are.

THE PASSION OF SPEECH/1

Marcela was visiting the snowy North. One night in Oslo, she met a woman who sang and told stories. Between songs, she would spin yarns, glancing at slips of paper like someone telling fortunes from crib notes.

This woman from Oslo had on an enormous dress dotted all over with pockets. She would pull slips of paper out of her pockets one by one, each with its story to tell, stories tried and true of people who wished to come back to life through witchcraft. And so she raised the dead and the forgotten, and from the depths of her dress sprang the odysseys and loves of the human animal for whom speech is life.

This man, or woman, is pregnant with many people. People are coming out of his pores. With these clay figures, the Hopi Indians of New Mexico depict the story teller: the one who relates the collective memory, who fairly blossoms with little people.

THE HOUSE OF WORDS

Helena Villagra dreamed that the poets were entering the house of words. The words, kept in old glass bottles, waited for the poets, and offered themselves, mad with desire to be chosen: they begged the poets to look at them, smell them, touch them, lick them. The poets opened the bottles, tried words on their fingertips and smacked their lips or wrinkled their noses. The poets were in search of words they didn't know as well as words they did know and had lost.

In the house of words was a table of colors. They offered themselves in great fountains and each poet took the color he needed: lemon yellow or sun yellow, ocean blue or smoke blue, crimson red, blood red, wine red . . .

THE FUNCTION OF
THE READER/1

When Lucía Peláez was very small, she read a novel under the covers. She read it in fragments, night after night, hiding it under the pillow. She had stolen it from the cedar bookshelf where her uncle kept his favorite books.

As the years passed, Lucía traveled far.

In search of phantoms, she walked over the rocks in the Antioquía River, and in search of people, she walked the streets of the violent cities.

Lucía walked a long way, and in the course of her travels was always accompanied by echoes of the echoes of those distant voices she had heard with her eyes when she was small.

Lucía has never read that book again. She would no longer recognize it. It has grown so much inside her that now it is something else: now it is hers.

THE FUNCTION OF
THE READER/2

It was half a century since the death of César Vallejo, and there were celebrations. In Spain, Julio Vélez organized lectures, seminars, memorial publications and an exhibition offering images of the poet, his land, his time and his people.

But then Julio Vélez met José Manuel Castañón, and all homage seemed insignificant.

José Manuel Castañón had been a captain in the Spanish War. Fighting for Franco, he had lost a hand and won various medals.

One night, shortly after the war, the captain accidentally came upon a banned book. He took a look, he read one line, he read another, and he could no longer tear himself away. Captain Castañón, hero of the victorious army, sat up all night, captivated, reading and rereading César Vallejo, poet of the defeated. Next morning he resigned from the army and refused to take a single peseta more from the Franco government.

Later, they put him in jail, and he went into exile.

CELEBRATION OF
THE HUMAN VOICE/1

The Shuar Indians, also known as Jíbaros, would cut off the heads of their vanquished enemies. They would cut off and shrink their heads until they fit into the palm of the hand, to prevent the defeated warriors from coming back to life. But a vanquished enemy is not vanquished altogether until his mouth has been sealed. They sew his lips together with thread that never rots.

CELEBRATION OF
THE HUMAN VOICE/2

Their hands were tied or handcuffed, yet their fingers danced, flew, drew words. The prisoners were hooded, but leaning back, they could see a bit, just a bit, down below. Although it was forbidden to speak, they spoke with their hands. Pinio Ungerfeld taught me the finger alphabet, which he had learned in prison without a teacher:

"Some of us had bad handwriting," he told me. *"Others were masters of calligraphy."*

The Uruguayan dictatorship wanted everyone to stand alone, everyone to be no one: in prisons and barracks, and throughout the country, communication was a crime.

Some prisoners spent more than ten years buried in solitary cells the size of coffins, hearing nothing but clanging bars or footsteps in the corridors. Fernández Huidobro and Mauricio Rosencof, thus condemned, survived because they could talk to each other by tapping on the wall. In that way they told of dreams and memories, fallings in and out of love; they discussed, embraced, fought; they shared beliefs and beauties, doubts and guilts, and those questions that have no answer.

When it is genuine, when it is born of the need to speak, no one can stop the human voice. When denied a mouth, it speaks with the hands or the eyes, or the pores, or anything at all. Because every single one of us has something to say to the others, something that deserves to be celebrated or forgiven by others.

A DEFINITION OF ART

"Portinari isn't here," said Portinari. He poked his nose out for an instant, slammed the door and disappeared.

This was in the thirties, the years of communist witch hunts in Brazil, and Portinari had exiled himself in Montevideo.

Iván Kmaid was not of those years nor of that place, but long afterward, he appeared through the holes in the curtain of time and told me what he had seen: Candido Portinari painted from morning to evening, and at night as well.

"Portinari isn't here," he would say.

At that time, communist intellectuals in Uruguay were going to take a position on social realism and wanted their prestigious comrade's opinion.

"We know you're not there," they said to him, and implored: *"But won't you give us a moment? Just a moment."*

And they posed the question.

"I don't know," said Portinari.

And then:

"All I know is this: art is art, or it's shit."

THE LANGUAGE OF ART

Chinolope sold papers and shined shoes in Havana. To escape poverty, he went to New York.

There, somebody gave him an old camera. Chinolope had never held a camera in his hands, but they told him it was easy:

"You just look through here and press there."

So he took to the streets. He hadn't been walking long when he heard shots. He went into a barbershop, raised the camera, looked through here and pressed there.

In the barbershop they had shot down the gangster Albert Anastasia while he was getting a shave, and that was the first photo of Chinolope's professional life.

He was paid a fortune. The photo was a coup. Chinolope had managed to photograph death. Death was there: not in the dead man, nor in the killer. Death was in the face of the barber looking on.

THE LIMITS OF ART

It was the longest of many battles fought in Tuscatlán or any other part of El Salvador. It began at midnight when the first grenades fell from the hillside, and lasted all night until the evening of the next day. The military said that Cinquera was impregnable. Four times the guerrillas had attacked and four times they had failed. The fifth time, when the white flag was raised over the command post, shots fired into the air signaled the beginning of the celebrations.

Julio Ama, who fought and photographed the war, wandered through the streets. He had a rifle in his hand and a camera, also loaded and ready to shoot, around his neck. He went through the dusty streets in search of the twin brothers. The twins were the only survivors of a village exterminated by the army. They were sixteen years old. They liked to fight alongside Julio, and between engagements he would teach them to read and take photographs. In the tumult of the battle, Julio had lost the twins and now could not find them among either the living or the dead.

He walked across the park. At the corner by the church, he entered a lane. And there, finally, he found them. One of

them was sitting on the ground, his back against a wall. The other lay across his knees, bathed in blood. At their feet, in the form of a cross, were their two rifles.

Julio approached—perhaps said something. The living twin neither spoke nor moved. He was there and he wasn't there. His unblinking eyes stared without seeing, lost somewhere, nowhere, and that tearless face was the whole of war, the whole of pain.

Julio left his rifle on the ground and gripped the camera. He advanced the film, calculated the light and distance in a flash, and focused. The brothers were centered in his viewfinder, motionless, perfectly profiled against the wall newly peppered with bullet holes.

Julio was about to take the picture of his life, but his finger refused. Julio tried, tried again, and his finger refused. Then he lowered the camera without releasing the shutter, and retreated in silence.

The camera, a Minolta, died in another battle, drowned by the rain a year later.

THE FUNCTION OF ART/2

The preacher Miguel Brun told me that a few years ago he had visited the Indians of the Paraguayan Chaco. He was part of an evangelizing mission. The missionaries visited a chief who was considered very wise. The chief, a quiet, fat man, listened without blinking to the religious propaganda that they read to him in his own language. When they finished, the missionaries awaited a reaction.

The chief took his time, then said:

"That scratches. It scratches hard and it scratches very well."

And then he added:

"But it scratches where there isn't any itch."

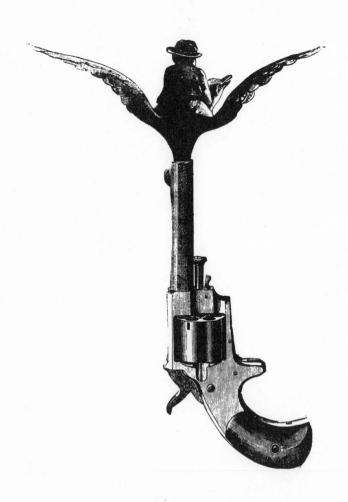

PROPHECIES/1

In Peru, a soothsayer covered me with red roses and then told my fortune. She announced:

"Within a month you will receive a distinction."

I laughed. I laughed for the infinite goodness of this stranger who was giving me flowers and auguries of success. And I laughed at the word "distinction," finding it a little ridiculous, and because I flashed back to an old neighborhood friend who was very crude but always on the mark, and who used to say, passing sentence as he raised his finger:

"Sooner or later, every writer gets hamburgerized." *

So I laughed, and the soothsayer laughed at my laughter.

One month later, to the day, I received a telegram in Montevideo. In Chile, the telegram said, I had been awarded a *distinction*. It was the José Carrasco prize.

---

*Se hamburquesan: in Spanish a play on the words *hamburquesa,* hamburger, and *burques,* bourgeois.

CELEBRATION OF
THE HUMAN VOICE/3

José Carrasco was a journalist for the magazine *Análisis*. Early
one morning, in the spring of 1986, he was dragged from his
house. A few hours earlier, an attempt had been made on the
life of General Augusto Pinochet, and a few days earlier, the
dictator had said:

"We are keeping an eye on certain gentlemen."

At the foot of a wall on the edge of Santiago, they put
fourteen bullets into his head. It was early morning, and
nobody was to be seen. His body lay there on the ground
until midday.

The neighbors never washed the blood away. The place
became a sanctuary for the poor, always strewn with candles
and flowers, and José Carrasco became a miracle worker. On
the wall pitted by the shots, one can read thanks for favors
received.

At the beginning of 1988, I traveled to Chile. It had been
fifteen years since I was last there. I was received at the airport
by Juan Pablo Cárdenas, editor of the magazine.

Condemned for offences against the government, Cárdenas
slept in prison. He entered the prison every night at exactly
ten o'clock, and left with the sunrise.

CHRONICLE OF THE CITY
OF SANTIAGO

Santiago de Chile, like other Latin American cities, has a glowing face. For less than a dollar a day, legions of workers polish the mask.

In the high-class districts people live as they do in Miami; they *do* live in Miami; life is Miamified, plastic clothing, plastic food, plastic people, and videos and computers are synonymous with happiness.

But there are ever fewer of these Chileans, and ever more of the other Chileans, the sub-Chileans. The economy curses them, the police chase them and the culture denies their existence.

Some became beggars. Flouting the prohibitions, they manage to appear beneath red traffic lights or in any doorway. There are beggars of all sizes and colors, whole and crippled, sincere and simulated, some in total desperation and on the edge of madness, others displaying twisted faces and trembling hands which they have rehearsed well: admirable professionals, veritable artists of fine begging.

At the height of the military dictatorship, the best of the Chilean beggars was one who moved his prey to pity saying: *"I'm a civilian."*

NERUDA/1

I was in Isla Negra, in the house that was, that is, Pablo Neruda's.

No one was allowed to go in. A wooden fence surrounded the house. On it people had written their messages to the poet. Not an inch of wood was left bare. They all spoke to him as if he were alive. With pencils or the points of nails, each had found a way to thank him.

I also found a way, without words. And I entered without entering. We were silently chatting about wines, the poet and I, talking quietly of oceans and of loves, and of an infallible remedy for baldness. We shared some shrimp pil-pil and a prodigious crab pie and other marvels that make the soul and belly—which, as he well knows, are just two different names for the same thing—rejoice.

We raised our glasses of fine wine time and again, and a salty wind whipped our faces. It was all a ceremony of malediction against the dictatorship, that black spear sticking in his side, that sonofabitch pain, and it was also a ceremony in celebration of life—beautiful and ephemeral as altars of flowers and passing loves.

NERUDA / 2

It happened in La Sebastiana, another of Neruda's homes, on the mountainside overlooking the bay of Valparaiso. The house had been uninhabited for a long time, sealed tight with stone, crossbars, lock and key.

The military had seized power, blood had flowed through the streets, Neruda had died of cancer—or grief. Then strange sounds inside the walled up house drew the attention of the neighbors. Someone looked through a high window and saw an inexplicable eagle with gleaming eyes, its claws extended for attack. The eagle could not have been there, could not have entered—there was no way in—but there it was, inside; and there, inside the house, it was violently flapping its wings.

PROPHECIES/2

Helena dreamed about the keepers of the fire. The poorest old women had stored it away in suburban kitchens and had only to blow very gently on their palms to rekindle the flame.

CELEBRATION OF FANTASY

It happened at the entrance to the town of Ollantaytambo, near Cuzco. I had detached myself from a group of tourists and was standing alone looking at the stone ruins in the distance when a small boy from the neighborhood, skinny and ragged, came over to ask if I would give him a pen. I couldn't give him my pen because I was using it to write down all sorts of boring notes, but I offered to draw a little pig for him on his hand.

Suddenly the word got around. I was surrounded by a throng of little boys demanding at the top of their lungs that I draw animals on their little hands cracked by the dirt and cold, their skin of burnt leather: one wanted a condor and one a snake, others preferred little parrots and owls, and some asked for a ghost or a dragon.

Then, in the middle of this racket, a little waif who barely cleared a yard off the ground showed me a watch drawn in black ink on his wrist.

"An uncle of mine who lives in Lima sent it to me," he said.

"And does it keep good time?" I asked him.

"It's a bit slow," he admitted.

ART FOR CHILDREN

She was seated in a high chair before a plate of soup at eye level. Her nose was wrinkled, her teeth clenched, and her arms crossed. Her mother pleaded for help:

"Tell her a story, Onelio," she implored. *"You're the writer. Tell her a story."*

And flourishing a spoonful of soup, Onelio Jorge Cardoso, began his story:

"There once was a birdy that didn't want to eat her dinny. The birdy had her beaky shut tight and her mommy said to her 'You're always going to be a tiny little birdy if you don't eat your din-din.' But the birdy didn't pay attention to her mommy and didn't open her beaky . . ."

Then the child broke in:

"What a shitty little birdy," she said.

CHILDREN'S OWN ART

Mario Montenegro sings the stories his children tell him.

He sits on the floor with his guitar in a circle of kids and the kids—or rabbits—tell him the story of the seventy rabbits who climbed on top of each other to kiss the giraffe; or they tell him the story of the blue rabbit who was all alone in the middle of the sky: a star took the blue rabbit for a walk around the sky and they visited the moon, which is a big white round land all full of holes and they spun around in space and jumped on the cottony clouds, and then the star got tired and went back to the land of stars, and the rabbit went back to the land of rabbits, and there he ate corn and shat and went to sleep and dreamed that he was a blue rabbit all alone in the middle of the sky.

HELENA'S DREAMS

That night a line formed of dreams wishing to be dreamed, but it was not possible for Helena to dream them all. One of them, a dream she didn't recognize, pressed its case:

"Dream me—I'll be worth your while. Dream me—you're going to like me."

Several new dreams that had never before been dreamed got on line, but Helena recognized the dopey dream that kept coming back, the dull dream, and other funny or gloomy dreams that were old friends of hers from nights of high flying.

JOURNEY TO THE LAND
OF DREAMS

Helena was traveling in a horse-drawn carriage to the land
where dreams are dreamed. Her puppy, Pepa Lumpen, was
sitting by her side in the coachman's seat. Under her arm,
Pepa carried a hen that was going to work in her dream.
Helena had brought along an enormous chest full of masks
and multicolored rags.

The road was crawling with people. They were all on their
way to the land of dreams, and were causing such a scandal
and making such a racket as they rehearsed their dreams that
Pepa did nothing but grumble, because she couldn't concen-
trate properly.

THE LAND OF DREAMS

It was a huge camp out in the country.

Singing heads of lettuce and luminous chilies sprouted from magicians' top hats and there were people all over bartering dreams. One wanted to trade a travel dream for a love dream and another offered a dream to make you laugh for a dream to give you a good cry.

One man wandered around in search of the pieces of his dream, shattered by someone who had got in his way. He was picking up the pieces and sticking them together to make a multicolored flag.

The dream water boy brought water to those who got thirsty as they slept. He carried the water on his back in a clay vessel and dispensed it in tall glasses.

There was a woman in a tower wearing a white tunic and combing her tresses, which reached down to her feet. The comb shed dreams replete with all their characters: the dreams flew from her hair into the air.

FORGOTTEN DREAMS

Helena dreamed she had left her forgotten dreams on an island.

Claribel Alegría gathered Helena's dreams together, tied them up with a ribbon, and put them away for safekeeping. But her children discovered the hiding place and wanted to try on Helena's dreams. Claribel told them very crossly:

"Don't even touch them."

Then she called Helena on the phone and asked her:

"What should I do with your dreams?"

THE DREAMS TAKE
THEIR LEAVE

The dreams were off on a trip. Helena went as far as the train station with them. She bade them farewell from the platform, waving a handkerchief.

CELEBRATION OF REALITY

If Dámaso Murúa's aunt had told her story to García Márquez, perhaps *Chronicle of a Death Foretold* would have had a different ending.

In her good days, Susana Contreras—that was the name of Dámaso's aunt—possessed the most incendiary ass ever seen blazing in the town of Escuinapa or anywhere around the Gulf of California.

Years ago, Susana married one of the many gallants who succumbed to her swinging hips. On the wedding night, her husband discovered that she was not a virgin. So he threw off the ardent Susana as if she were infected with the plague, slammed the door, and left for good.

The indignant bridegroom started drinking in the cantinas, where wedding guests were continuing their binge. Embracing his friends he began muttering resentful remarks and making threats, but no one took his cruel torment seriously. They listened to him benevolently as, in macho fashion, he swallowed back the tears that welled up in his eyes. But then they told him that it was hardly news, that of course Susana wasn't a virgin, that the whole town knew it except for him, and that after all, it was a detail of no importance whatsoever, and don't be an idiot, man, you only live once. He persisted, but instead of gestures of solidarity, received only yawns.

And so the night, progressing in a sad and increasingly solitary drinking spree, lurched toward dawn. One by one the guests went off to sleep. Morning found the offended man sitting in the street, totally alone and quite exhausted from so much groaning without anybody paying any attention to him.

By now he was growing bored with his own tragedy, and the first light of day dispelled his craving for suffering and vengeance. At mid-morning he took a nice bath and downed a good hot cup of coffee and by noon he was returning, contrite, to the arms of the spurned woman.

He came in a procession of marchers, high-stepping from the far end of the main street. He carried an enormous bouquet of roses and led a parade of friends, relatives, and the general public. A band brought up the rear. They were playing their hearts out, playing for Susana—by way of repentance—*"La negra consentida"* and *"Vereda tropical."* It was with these very tunes that he had not long before declared his passion.

ART AND REALITY/1

Fernando Birri was going to film the story of the angel by García Márquez, and he took me to see the set. On the Cuban coast, Fernando had established a little cardboard village and filled it with chickens, giant crabs, and actors. He was to play the lead role, that of the deplumed angel who falls to earth and is shut up in a henhouse.

Marcial, a local fisherman, had been solemnly appointed magistrate of the filmtown. After the official greeting, Marcial accompanied us. Fernando wanted to show me a masterpiece of artificial aging: a rickety, leprous, beaten up cage, corroded with rust and ancient dirt. This was to be the angel's prison after his flight from the henhouse. But instead of this cage, artfully ruined by the specialists, we found a clean cage in fine condition, its bars perfectly aligned and recently painted gold. Marcial puffed up with pride as he showed us this marvel. Fernando, half astonished and half furious, nearly ate him alive.

"What is this Marcial? What's this?"

Marcial was dumbfounded. He turned red, hung his head, and scratched his belly. Then he confessed:

"I couldn't permit it. I couldn't allow them to put a good man like you in that disgusting cage."

Eraclio Zepeda played the role of Pancho Villa in *Insurgent Mexico,* the film by Paul Leduc, and he played it so well that ever since, some people think Eraclio Zepeda is the name Pancho Villa uses when he works in the movies.

They were in the middle of making this film, in some little village, and the people were participating in everything in the most natural way without the director having to say a word. Pancho Villa had been dead for half a century, but it surprised no one that he should appear around there. One night after an intensive day's work, some women gathered before the house where Eraclio was sleeping and asked him to intercede on behalf of some locals in prison. The next morning, bright and early, he went to talk to the mayor.

"General Villa had to come for justice to be done," the people commented.

REALITY IS MAD AS A HATTER

"*Tell me something. Tell me whether Marxism forbids eating glass. I'd like to know.*"

This happened in the mid-seventies, in the eastern part of Cuba. The man was standing in the doorway, waiting. I begged his pardon. I said that I didn't know much about Marxism, just a little, a very little, and that he would be better off consulting a specialist in Havana.

"*They already took me to Havana,*" he said, "*where I was examined by doctors. The Comandante paid me a visit. Fidel said to me: 'Look here: Are you doing this simply out of ignorance?'*"

For eating glass, they took away his Communist Youth card.

"*They examined me right here in Baracoa.*"

Trígimo Suárez was an exemplary militiaman, a frontline sugar cane cutter and a vanguard worker—the kind who works twenty hours and charges for eight. He was always the first to step forward to cut cane or shoulder a gun, but he had a passion for glass.

"*It's not a defect,*" he explained to me. "*It's a need.*"

When Trígimo was mobilized to help with the harvest or to go on military exercises, his mother would pack his rucksack with food: she would put in a few empty bottles for lunch and dinner, and for dessert, old fluorescent tubes. She would also throw in some burnt out lightbulbs for him to snack on.

Trígimo took me to his house in Camilo Cienfuegos, a division of Baracoa. As we chatted, I drank coffee and he ate lightbulbs. When he finished off the glass, he sucked greedily on the filaments.

"*Glass calls to me. I love glass like I love the Revolution.*"

Trígimo assured me that he had no blots on his past. He had never eaten glass belonging to anyone else except once, just once, when, crazed with hunger, he devoured a fellow worker's eyeglasses.

CHRONICLE OF THE CITY OF HAVANA

His parents had fled to the north. In those days, he and the revolution were both in their infancy. A quarter of a century later, Nelson Valdés traveled from Los Angeles to Havana to visit his homeland.

Every day at noon, Nelson would take the *guagua,* bus number 68, from the hotel entrance, to the José Martí Library, There he would read books on Cuba until nightfall.

One day at noon, *guagua* 68 screeched to a halt at an intersection. There were cries of protest at the tremendous jolt until the passengers saw why the bus driver had jammed on the brakes: a magnificent woman had just crossed the street.

"You'll have to forgive me, gentlemen," said the driver of *guagua* 68, and he got out. All the passengers applauded and wished him luck.

The bus driver swaggered along, in no hurry, and the passengers watched him approach the saucy female, who stood on the corner, leaning against the wall, licking an ice cream cone. From *guagua* 68, the passengers followed the darting motion of her tongue as it kissed the ice cream while the driver talked on and on with no apparent result, until all

at once she laughed and glanced up at him. The driver gave
the thumbs-up sign and the passengers burst into a hearty
ovation.

But when the driver went into the ice cream parlor, the
passengers began to get restless. And when he came out a bit
later with an ice cream cone in each hand, panic spread among
the masses.

They beeped the horn. Someone leaned on it with all his
might and honked like a burglar alarm, but the bus driver,
deaf, nonchalant, was glued to the delectable woman.

Then, from the back of *guagua* 68, a woman with the
appearance of a huge cannon ball, and an air of authority,
stepped forward. Without a word, she sat in the driver's seat
and put the engine in gear. *Guagua* 68 continued on its route,
stopping at its customary stops, until the woman arrived at
her own and got off. Another passenger took her place for a
stretch, stopping at every bus stop, and then another, and
another, and so *guagua* 68 continued on to the end of the line.

Nelson Valdés was the last one to get off. He had forgotten
all about the library.

DIPLOMACY IN LATIN AMERICA

"W*hat is that?*" tourists would inquire.

Balmaceda would smile, apologize, and shake his head. Like everyone else, he had a garland of flowers around his neck and wore a Hawaiian shirt and sunglasses, but the leaden package he held in his hands had him sweating like a pig.

It seemed he was serving a life sentence. He had tried to jettison his enormous bundle in the bathroom of a hotel in Manila and on the inspection table at customs in Papeete. He had tried to throw it overboard on the boat and to mislay it in the lush island foliage of the Tahiti archipelago. But someone would always run after him:

"Sir! Sir! You've forgotten something!"

This sad tale began when Marcos, dictator of the Philip-

pines, invited Pinochet, dictator of Chile, for a visit. The
Chilean Ministry of Foreign Affairs sent along a bronze bust
of General O'Higgins from Santiago to Manila. Pinochet
planned to unveil the effigy of that illustrious figure in the
city's main square. But Marcos, frightened by the rage of the
people, suddenly canceled the invitation. Pinochet was forced
to return to Chile without even touching ground. This was
when Balmaceda, a minor official, received express orders in
the Chilean embassy in Manila. From Santiago they told him
over the phone:

*"Cut the rigmarole. Get rid of the bust any way you can. Bring
it back to Chile and you're out of a job."*

CHRONICLE OF THE CITY OF QUITO

He marches at the head of left-wing demonstrations. He often attends cultural parties although they bore him, because he knows there will be drinks afterwards. He likes his rum neat, but it must be Cuban.

He obeys traffic lights. He roams Quito from one end to the other, dropping in on friends and enemies alike. On steep hills, he prefers to take the bus but never pays the fare. Some of the drivers tell him off: *"Damn one-eye!"* they shout as he gets down.

His name is Choco and he is a troublemaker and a lover. He'll take on four adversaries at once, and when there is a full moon, he'll slip out in search of girlfriends. Later, all worked up, he recounts his wild adventures. Mishy doesn't catch the details but he gets the drift.

Once, years ago, he was taken far from Quito. Food was scarce and they had decided to return him to his distant birthplace. But he made it back. He was back in a month. He got to the door of his house and collapsed without the strength to celebrate his arrival with even a wag of his tail, or announce himself with a bark. He had crossed many mountains and avenues and had arrived on his last legs, a wreck, a sack of bones, his fur matted with dried blood. Ever since, he has loathed hats, uniforms, and motorcycles.

THE STATE IN LATIN AMERICA

It was quite a few years ago, ages ago, that Colonel Amen told me this.

It seems that a soldier received the order to change barracks. They sent him away for a year to some barracks on the border, because the government of Uruguay had begun one of its periodic wars on smuggling.

As he left, the soldier entrusted his wife and other belongings to the custody of his best friend.

A year later, he returned to find that his best friend, also a soldier, didn't want to give back the woman. There was no problem about returning the other things, but not the woman. The dispute was about to be settled by the verdict of the knife, a Creole duel, when Colonel Amen put a stop to it:

"Explain yourselves," he demanded.

"The woman is mine," said the man who had been away.

"His? She may have been his. But not any longer," said the other.

"Reasons," said the Colonel. *"I want reasons."*

And the usurper reasoned:

"But Colonel, how can I give her back to him? After all that poor woman has suffered? If you could have seen how this animal treated her. . . . He treated her, Colonel . . . as though she were the property of the State!"

BUREAUCRACY/1

In the days of the military dictatorship, in the middle of 1973, a Uruguayan political prisoner, Juan José Noueched, received a five-day punishment: five days without visitation rights or exercise; five days without anything, for having violated the rule. From the point of view of the captain who imposed the punishment, the rule left no room for argument. The rule clearly established that prisoners must walk single file with both hands behind their backs. Noueched had been punished for putting only one hand behind his back.

Noueched was one-armed.

He had been taken prisoner in two stages. First, his arm was taken. Then he was. His arm was taken in Montevideo. Noueched was escaping as fast as his legs could carry him when the policeman chasing him managed to grab him and shout: *"You're under arrest!"* and found himself holding the arm. The rest of Noueched was taken a year and a half later, in Paysandú.

In prison, Noueched wanted his lost arm back:

"Fill out a request form," they told him.

He explained that he didn't have a pencil:

"Fill out a request for a pencil," they told him.

Then he had a pencil, but no paper:

"Fill out a request for paper," they told him.

When at last he had pencil and paper, he wrote out a request for his arm.

Eventually, he got an answer. No. It wasn't possible: his arm was under different jurisdiction. He had been tried in a military court. His arm had been tried as a civilian.

BUREAUCRACY/2

Tito Sclavo managed to see and transcribe some official documents in the prison called Liberty during the years of the Uruguayan dictatorship. They were rules for punishment: prisoners committing the crime of drawing birds or couples or pregnant women, or those caught using flowered towels, were sentenced to solitary confinement. One prisoner, who like everyone else had his head shaved clean, was punished *"for entering the dining room uncombed."* Another *"for sticking his head under the door"*—though one millimeter of light passed beneath the door. Solitary confinement also awaited the prisoner who *"tried to befriend a military dog"* and another who *"insulted a dog who was a member of the Armed Forces."* Another earned the same reward for *"barking like a dog for no good reason."*

BUREAUCRACY/3

Sixto Martínez completed his military service at a barracks in Seville.

In the middle of the courtyard of that barracks was a small bench. Next to the small bench, a soldier stood guard. No one knew why the bench had to be guarded. The bench was guarded around the clock, just because: every day, every night, and from one generation of officers to the next the order was passed on and the soldiers obeyed it. No one expressed any doubts or ever asked why. If that's how it was done, and that's how it had always been done, there had to be a reason.

And so it continued until someone, some general or colonel, wanted to look at the original order. He had to rummage through all the files. After a good deal of poking around, he found the answer. Thirty-one years, two months and four days ago, an officer had ordered a guard to be stationed beside the small bench, which had just been painted, so that no one would think of sitting on the wet paint.

HAPPENINGS/1

By the hearths of Paysandú, Mellado Iturria relates what has happened in the world. These happenings happened at one time or another, or almost did, or never did, but their virtue is that they happen every time they are told.

This is the sad story of the little catfish of Negro Brook.

He had pointy whiskers and crossed, bulging eyes. Mellado had never seen such an ugly fish in all his life. The catfish followed on his heels from the brook's edge, and Mellado could not shake him. By the time he got home, the catfish trailing him like his own shadow, he had resigned himself.

As time went by, he began to take a liking to the catfish. Mellado had never had a friend without legs. At daybreak the catfish would go with him to milk the cows and inspect the fields. At the close of day, they would drink *mate* together, and the catfish would listen to Mellado's deepest secrets.

The jealous dogs eyed the catfish with resentment; the

cooks with bad intentions. Mellado considered naming him
so he could call the catfish and get him to show a little respect,
but he couldn't think of any fish names and God might not be
pleased by a name like Sinforoso or Hermenegildo.

He didn't let the fish out of his sight. It had the scandalous
habit of getting into all kinds of mischief. Whenever Mellado
wasn't looking, it would go frighten the hens or needle the
dogs.

"Behave yourself," Mellado would tell him.

One broiling morning when the lizards were out with
their parasols and the little catfish was fanning itself with its
fins for all it was worth, Mellado had a tragic idea:

"Let's take a dip in the brook," he suggested.

So off they went.

The catfish drowned.

HAPPENINGS/2

In the old days, Don Verídico planted houses and people all around his saloon "The Resort," so that it would not stand alone. This happened, so they say, in the town created by his own hand.

And they also say that there was treasure there, hidden in the house of a feeble old man.

Once a month, the old man, who was nearing his end, would get out of bed and go collect his pension.

Taking advantage of his absence, some thieves from Montevideo broke into his house.

The thieves searched every nook and cranny for the treasure. All they found was a wooden chest covered with blankets in one corner of the cellar. The enormous padlock that secured it resisted the lockpickers' attack undefeated.

So they made off with the chest. When they opened it far from the house, they found that it was filled with letters. They were the love letters the old man had received throughout the course of his long life.

The thieves were going to burn the letters. They talked it over. Finally they decided to return them. One by one. One a week. Since then, every Monday at noon, the old man sat high on the hill and waited for the postman to appear down the road. As soon as he saw the horse, fat with saddlebags, emerge from among the trees, the old man started running. The postman, who knew all about it, held the letter in his hand.

And even St. Peter could hear the beating of that heart, crazed with joy of receiving woman's words.

HAPPENINGS/3

What is truth? Truth is a lie told by Fernando Silva.

Fernando tells stories not only with words but with his whole body. He can turn himself into someone else or into a flying critter or anything at all, and he does it in such a way that afterwards one hears, let us say, a mockingbird singing in a tree, and thinks:

"That bird is imitating Fernando imitating a mockingbird."

He tells stories of the beautiful little people: newly created people still smelling of clay; and also of outrageous characters he has known—like the mirror-maker who made mirrors he would walk into and get lost in, or the volcano-snuffer whom the Devil blinded in one eye out of vengeance by spitting in it. The stories happen in places where Fernando has been: the hotel open only to ghosts, the mansion where witches died of boredom, or Ticuantepe's house, which was so dark and cool one longed to have a girlfriend waiting there.

In addition, Fernando works as a doctor. He prefers herbs to pills, and cures ulcers with *cardosanto* and pigeons' eggs; but prefers his own hands to herbs. For he cures by the laying on of hands—and by telling stories, which is another way of laying on hands.

CHRISTMAS EVE

Fernando Silva ran the children's hospital in Managua. On Christmas Eve, he worked late into the night. Firecrackers were exploding and fireworks lit up the sky when Fernando decided it was time to leave. They were expecting him at home to celebrate the holiday.

He took one last look around, checking to see that everything was in order, when he heard cottony footsteps behind him. He turned to find one of the sick children walking after him. In the half light he recognized the lonely, doomed child. Fernando recognized that face already lined with death and those eyes asking for forgiveness, or perhaps permission.

Fernando walked over to him and the boy gave him his hand.

"Tell someone, . . ." the child whispered. *"Tell someone I'm here."*

THE NOBODIES

Fleas dream of buying themselves a dog, and nobodies dream of escaping poverty: that one magical day good luck will suddenly rain down on them—will rain down in buckets. But good luck doesn't rain down yesterday, today, tomorrow, or ever. Good luck doesn't even fall in a fine drizzle, no matter how hard the nobodies summon it, even if their left hand is tickling, or if they begin the new day with their right foot, or start the new year with a change of brooms.

The nobodies: nobody's children, owners of nothing. The nobodies: the no ones, the nobodied, running like rabbits, dying through life, screwed every which way.

Who are not, but could be.

Who don't speak languages, but dialects.

Who don't have religions, but superstitions.

Who don't create art, but handicrafts.

Who don't have culture, but folklore.

Who are not human beings, but human resources.

Who do not have faces, but arms.

Who do not have names, but numbers.

Who do not appear in the history of the world, but in the police blotter of the local paper.

The nobodies, who are not worth the bullet that kills them.

HUNGER / 1

Leaving San Salvador and heading toward Guazapa, Berta Navarro met a peasant woman displaced by the war. She was no different from any of the other women and men who had exchanged hunger for starvation. But this scraggly, ugly peasant woman was standing in the midst of desolation, her skin hanging loose on her bones and a scraggly, ugly little bird in her hand. The bird was dead and she was very slowly plucking its feathers.

CHRONICLE OF THE CITY OF CARACAS

"*I need someone to listen to me!*" he shouted.

"*They always tell me to come back tomorrow!*" he shouted.

He threw down his shirt. Then his socks and shoes.

José Manuel Pereira was standing on the cornice of the eighteenth floor of a building in Caracas.

The police tried to grab him but failed.

A psychologist talked to him from the nearest window.

Then a priest brought him the word of God.

"*I'm sick of promises!*" José Manuel shouted.

He could be seen through the picture windows of the restaurant in the South Tower, standing on the cornice with his hands flat against the wall. It was lunchtime and he was the topic of conversation at every table.

Down at street level, a crowd had gathered.

Six hours passed.

The crowd finally grew tired of waiting.

"Why doesn't he make up his mind?" people were saying.

"Why doesn't he just jump?" people were thinking.

The firemen inched a rope over to him. At first, he ignored it. But finally he stretched out one hand, then the other, and holding onto the rope, he slid down to the sixteenth floor. Then, while trying to enter an open window, he slipped and plummeted through the air. When his body hit the pavement it made a sound like a bomb exploding.

Then the crowd dispersed, and the ice cream vendors and the hot dog vendors and the beer and soda vendors all continued on their way.

ADVERTISEMENTS

For sale:

- *One halfbreed negress of the Cabinda race, for the sum of 430 pesos. Knows rudiments of sewing and ironing.*
- *Leeches, recently arrived from Europe: prime quality. Four, five, and six* vintenes *apiece.*
- *Carriage. Will sell for five hundred* patacones, *or exchange for one negress.*
- *One negress, thirteen or fourteen years old, free of vices; of the Bangala race.*
- *Small mulatto, eleven years old, knows rudiments of tailoring.*
- *Essence of sarsaparilla, two pesos per bottle.*
- *One nursing female. To be sold without offspring, has good and plentiful milk.*
- *A lion, tame as a dog, will eat anything; a bureau and chest, both of mahogany.*
- *Maid, free of vices and disease, of the Conga race, approximately eighteen years of age; also, a piano and other pieces of furniture, all at reasonable prices.*

(From Uruguayan newspapers of 1840, twenty-seven years after the abolition of slavery.)

CHRONICLE OF THE CITY OF RÍO

In the middle of the Río de Janeiro night, the Hunchbacked Christ stands, luminous and generous, with outstretched arms. The grandchildren of slaves find refuge beneath those arms.

A barefoot woman looks up at Christ from far below and, pointing at the shining light, says with great sadness:

"He won't be there much longer. I hear they're taking him away."

"Don't worry," the woman next door assures her. *"Don't worry: He'll return."*

Many people are killed by the police, and many more by the economy. Drums as well as gunshots echo through the violent city: the drums, impatient for consolation and vengeance, call to the African gods. Christ alone is not enough.

THOSE LITTLE NUMBERS
AND PEOPLE

Where do people earn the Per Capita Income? More than one poor starving soul would like to know.

In our countries, numbers live better than people. How many people prosper in times of prosperity? How many people find their lives developed by development?

The Cuban Revolution triumphed during the year of greatest affluence in the history of that island.

In Central America, the more wretched and desperate the people, the more the statistics smiled and laughed. During the fifties, sixties and seventies, stormy decades, turbulent times, Central America boasted the highest economic growth rates in the world and the most extensive regional development in the history of human civilization.

In Colombia, rivers of blood merge with rivers of gold. Glories of the economy, years of cheap money: in the midst of euphoria, the country produces cocaine, coffee and crime in insane quantities.

HUNGER/2

A system of isolation: *Look out for number one.* Your neighbor is neither your brother nor your lover. Your neighbor is a competitor, an enemy, an obstacle to clear or an object to use. The system feeds neither the body nor the heart: many are condemned to starve for lack of bread and many more for lack of embraces.

CHRONICLE OF THE CITY OF NEW YORK

It is late night and I am at the southern tip of Manhattan, far from my hotel. I flag down a cab. I give the driver the address in perfect English, dictated perhaps by the ghost of my Liverpudlian great grandfather. The driver responds in perfect Guayaquil Spanish.

He puts the taxi in gear and begins to tell me the story of his life. Once he has started, he doesn't pause. He speaks without looking at me, his eyes glued to the river of headlights and brakelights along the avenue. He tells me of the times he's been held up and the times they've wanted to kill him and the insanity of New York City traffic, and the dizzying rhythm of buy, buy, consume, discard, be bought, be consumed, be discarded; that in this city you have to use brute force to get anywhere—step on the other guy or be stepped on: he'll walk right over you—and that he's been living this life since he was a child, you heard it right, since he was a child fresh from Ecuador—and he tells me that his woman just walked out on him.

His woman walked out on him after twelve years of marriage. It's not her fault, he says. It's over as soon as I get in, he says. She never enjoyed it, he says.

He says it's his prostate.

THE WALLS SPEAK/1

In the children's section of the Bogotá Book Fair:
The lunicopter is very swift, yet very slow.
On the boulevard of Montevideo beside the estuary:
Winged men prefer the night.
Leaving Santiago de Cuba:
How I cover the walls remembering you.
And in the heights of Valparaíso:
I love us.

LOVING

We made love spinning through space, a savory, saucy ball of flesh, a lone, hot little ball shining and steaming with juicy aromas as it turned and turned through Helena's dream and through the infinite void and fell as it spun, gently falling to the bottom of a huge bowl of salad. There it lay, the little ball that was the two of us, and from the bottom of the bowl we could glimpse the sky. With great effort, we made our way through the dense lettuce foliage, the branches of celery and the parsley forest, and could make out a few stars sailing in the farthest reaches of the night.

THEOLOGY/1

When I was very young, the catechism taught me to do good for the sake of convenience and not to do evil for fear of the consequences. God offered me punishments and rewards: he threatened me with hell and promised me heaven. And I feared and believed.

Time has gone by. I am neither afraid nor a believer. And anyway, it seems to me that if I deserve to be roasted on a spit over a slow, eternal flame, so it will be. That way I'll escape purgatory, which will be packed with dreadful middle-class tourists, and in the end, justice will be done.

Frankly, as deserving goes, I deserve it. I have never killed anyone, it's true, but for lack of courage or time, not for lack of desire. I don't go to Mass on Sundays or days of obligation. I have coveted almost all of my neighbor's women, except for the ugly ones, and thus have desecrated, at least in my heart, the private property that God himself sanctified in Moses' tables: *Thou shalt not covet thy neighbor's wife, or his ox, or his ass....* And to top it all, I have, with premeditation and in cold blood, committed the act of love without the noble intention of reproducing the labor force. I am acutely aware that carnal sins are very poorly regarded in heaven, but I suspect that God damns what he does not know.

THEOLOGY/2

The god of the Christians, God of my childhood, does not
make love. He is perhaps the only god that has never made
love out of all the gods of all the religions in the history of
the world. Whenever this occurs to me, I feel sorry for him.
And then I forgive him for having been my superfather cas-
tigator, chief of police of the universe, and I think that when
all is said and done, God also knew how to be my friend in
the old days when I believed in Him and believed that He
believed in me. Then I prick up my ears at the time of day
when the world is filled with magical rustlings, between the
setting of the sun and the fall of night, and I seem to hear his
melancholy confidences.

THEOLOGY/3

Errata: where the Old Testament says what it says, perhaps it should say what its main protagonist has confessed to me:

A pity that Adam was so stupid. A pity that Eve was so deaf. A pity that I didn't know how to make myself understood.

Adam and Eve were the first human beings made by my hand and I realize that they had certain defects in structure, assembly, and finish. They were not ready to listen, or to think. And I . . . well, maybe I was not ready to speak. Before Adam and Eve, I had never talked to anybody. I had pronounced grand phrases, like "Let there be light," but always alone. So the day I met Adam and Eve in the cool of the evening, I wasn't very eloquent. I lacked practice.

My first feeling was that of astonishment. They had just stolen the fruit from the forbidden tree in the center of Paradise. Adam had assumed the expression of a general about to surrender his sword, and Eve was staring at the ground as if counting ants. But they were both incredibly young and beautiful and radiant. They surprised me. I had made them, but I didn't know that mud could look so luminous.

Later, I admit, I felt envy. Just as no one can give me orders, I know nothing of the dignity of disobedience. Nor can I know the boldness of love, which requires two. In keeping with the principle of authority, I resisted the desire to congratulate them for having suddenly grown wise in human passion.

Then came the misunderstandings. They understood *"fall"* where I spoke of *"flight."* They thought that a sin deserved punishment if it was original. I said that those who fail to love are sinners; they understood that those who love are sinners. Where I spoke of a meadow of joy they understood a vale of tears. I said that pain was the salt that gave flavor to the human adventure; they understood that I was condemning them by granting them the glory of being mortal and a little nuts. They got everything backwards. And they believed it.

Lately, I've been suffering from insomnia. For several millennia now, I've been having trouble falling asleep. And I like sleeping, I really do, because when I sleep, I dream. Then I become a lover, I burn myself in the brief flame of fleeting love, I am a strolling player, a deep-sea fisherman, or a Gypsy fortune teller; I devour even the leaves of the forbidden tree and drink and dance until I'm rolling on the ground.

When I wake up, I am alone. I have no one to play with because the angels take me so seriously, nor have I anyone to desire. I am condemned to desire myself. I wander from star to star, growing bored in the empty universe. I feel very tired, I feel very alone. I am alone—alone for all eternity.

THE NIGHT/1

I can't sleep. There is a woman stuck between my eyelids. I would tell her to get out if I could. But there is a woman stuck in my throat.

DIAGNOSIS AND THERAPY

Love is among the most pernicious and contagious of diseases. We who are afflicted with it can be detected by anyone. Dark circles under our eyes show that we never sleep, kept awake night after night by embraces or by their absence. We suffer from devastating fevers and have an irresistible urge to say stupid things.

Love can be induced by dropping a pinch of loveme with feigned casualness into a cup of coffee or soup, or a drink. It can be induced but not prevented. Holy water does not prevent it, nor ground up host, and a clove of garlic is absolutely useless. Love is deaf to the divine Word and to witches' spells. No government decree has any power over it nor can any potion prevent it, although women in the market hawk infallible brews complete with guarantees.

THE NIGHT / 2

Woman, strip me of my clothes and my doubts. Undress me, undoubt me.

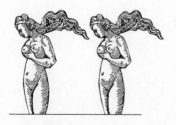

CALLINGS

The moon calls to the sea and the sea calls to the humble stream, which flows on and on from wherever it springs in search of the sea, no matter how far away it may lie, and growing as it flows, the stream rushes on until no mountain can hold back its surge. The sun calls to the grapevine, which spreads and rises in its hunger for sunlight. The early morning air calls forth the smells of the awakening city, the aroma of newly baked bread, of newly brewed coffee, and the aromas fill the air and possess it. Night calls to the water lily, and at the stroke of midnight those white points of light burst open in the river, opening the darkness, penetrating it, breaking it apart and swallowing it up.

THE NIGHT/3

I sleep on the rim of a woman: I sleep on the rim of a chasm.

A LITTLE DEATH

Love does not move us to laughter at the deepest point in its journey, the pinnacle of its flight: at its deepest and highest, it wrenches from us cries and moans, expressions of pain, however jubilant, which when you think about it is not strange at all because birth is a painful joy. *A little death* is what the French call the climax of the embrace, which joins us as it breaks us apart and finds us as it loses us, is our beginning as it is our end. *A little death* they call it, but it must be great, tremendous, to give birth to us as it kills us.

THE NIGHT/4

I break loose from the embrace, go forth into the street.
In the brightening sky, the moon is a fine sliver.
The moon is two nights old.
I, only one.

THE DEVOURER DEVOURED

The squid has the eyes of the fisherman who hooks him. The man who will be swallowed by the earth that feeds him is himself made of earth. The child eats its mother and earth eats sky every time it sucks rain from its breasts. The gluttonous flower closes over the beak of the bird, hungry for its honey. The awaited is also awaiting and the lover is both mouth and mouthful, devourer and devoured: lovers eat each other whole, from head to toe, every last bit, all-powerful, all-possessed, without leaving even the tip of an ear or the smallest toe.

THE WALLS SPEAK/2

In Buenos Aires on La Boca Bridge:
Everybody makes promises and nobody keeps them. Vote for nobody.

In Caracas, during a time of crisis, at the entrance to one of the poorest barrios:
Welcome, middle class.

In Bogotá, around the corner from the National University:
God lives.

And underneath, in a different hand:
By a sheer miracle.

And also in Bogotá:
Proletarians of all lands unite!

And underneath, in a different hand:
(Final notice.)

PROFESSIONAL LIFE/1

At the end of 1987, Héctor Abad Gómez reported that a man's life was worth no more than eight dollars. When his article was published in a Medellín daily, he had already been assassinated. Héctor Abad Gómez was president of the Commission on Human Rights.

In Colombia, it is rare to die of disease.

"How would you like the body, Your Excellency?"

The killer gets half on account. He loads the pistol and crosses himself. He prays to God to help him in his work.

Later, if his aim does not falter, he gets the other half. And in church, on his knees, he gives thanks for the divine grace.

CHRONICLE OF THE CITY OF BOGOTÁ

When the curtain fell each night, Patricia Ariza, marked for death, would close her eyes and silently give thanks for that night's applause and for having cheated death out of one more day of life.

Patricia was on the death list for thinking in red and living in red, and the sentences were being implacably carried out, one by one.

Finally, she was homeless. Worried that their building would be blown up, her neighbors, obeying the law of fear, demanded that she leave.

She walked the streets of Bogotá wearing a bulletproof vest. The vest was ugly and depressing, but she had no choice. One day, Patricia sewed some sequins onto it. Another day, she embroidered it with colorful flowers, a rain of flowers

over her breasts. And so, bit by bit, she embellished the vest, making it more and more cheerful, for like it or not, she was beginning to wear it wherever she went, even on stage.

When Patricia left Colombia to perform in Europe, she offered the vest to a peasant named Julio Cañón.

Julio Cañón, mayor of the town of Vistahermosa, had seen his whole family murdered as a warning, but he refused to wear the flowery vest:

"I don't wear women's clothing," he said.

With scissors, Patricia stripped the vest of its glitter and color. Then the man accepted her offer.

He was gunned down that night, wearing the vest.

IN PRAISE OF THE ART
OF ORATORY

There is a division of labor in the ranks of the powerful: the army, paramilitary organizations and hired assassins concern themselves with social contradictions and the class struggle. Civilians are responsible for speeches.

There are several speech factories in Bogotá although only one of them, the National Speech Factory, is listed in the phone book. These industrial mills have supplied numerous presidential campaigns in Colombia and neighboring countries, and regularly turn out speeches made to measure for parliamentary use, speeches to inaugurate schools or prisons, for weddings, birthdays or baptisms, to commemorate illustrious figures in the history of the nation, and to praise the deceased who leave in their wake a vacuum that can never be filled:

"I, perhaps the least qualified . . ."

PROFESSIONAL LIFE/2

They have the same first name, the same surname. They live in the same house and wear the same shoes. They sleep on the same pillow, next to the same woman. Every morning the mirror confronts them with the same face. But he and he are not the same person:

"And I, what have I got to do with it?" says he, speaking of him and shrugging his shoulders.

"I carry out orders," he says, or he says:

"That's what they pay me for."

Or he says:

"If I don't do it, someone else will."

Which is as if to say:

"I am someone else."

The hatred of the victim astonishes the executioner, and even leaves him feeling a certain sense of injustice: after all, he is an official, an ordinary official who goes to work on time and does his job. When the exhausting day's work is done, the torturer washes his hands.

Ahmadou Gherab, who fought for the independence of Algeria, told me this. Ahmadou was tortured by a French official for several months. Every day, promptly at 6:00 P.M, the torturer would wipe the sweat from his brow, unplug the electric cattle prod and put away the other tools of the trade. Then he would sit beside the tortured man and speak to him of his family problems and of the promotion that didn't come and of how expensive life is. The torturer would speak of his insufferable wife and their newborn child who had not permitted him a wink of sleep all night; he railed against Orán, that shitty city, and against the son of a bitch of a colonel who . . .

Ahmadou, bathed in blood, trembling with pain, burning with fever, would say nothing.

PROFESSIONAL LIFE/3

The big bankers of the world, who practice the terrorism of money, are more powerful than kings and field marshals, even more than the Pope of Rome himself. They never dirty their hands. They kill no one: they limit themselves to applauding the show.

Their officials, international technocrats, rule our countries: they are neither presidents nor ministers, they have not been elected, but they decide the level of salaries and public expenditure, investments and divestments, prices, taxes, interest rates, subsidies, when the sun rises and how frequently it rains.

However, they don't concern themselves with the prisons or torture chambers or concentration camps or extermination centers, although these house the inevitable consequences of their acts.

The technocrats claim the privilege of irresponsibility: *"We're neutral,"* they say.

MAPAMUNDI/1

The system:
It steals with one hand what it lends with the other.
Its victims:
The more they pay, the more they owe.
The more they get, the less they have.
The more they sell, the less they earn.

MAPAMUNDI/2

To the south, repression. To the north, depression.

More than a few northern intellectuals marry southern revolutions for the sheer pleasure of becoming widowers. They ostentatiously weep buckets, oceans of tears over the death of each illusion, and they never stop long enough to discover that socialism is the longest road from capitalism to capitalism.

It is fashionable in the north, throughout the world, to celebrate neutral art and applaud the snake that bites its tail and finds it tasty. Culture and politics have become consumer goods. Presidents are chosen on television like soap, and poets perform a decorative function. The only magic is that of the market, and bankers are the only heroes.

Democracy is a northern luxury. The south is permitted its show, which is denied to nobody. And in the final analysis, it doesn't bother anyone very much that politics be democratic so long as the economy is not. When the curtain falls, once the votes are deposited in the ballot boxes, reality imposes the law of might is right, which is the law of money, the pleasure of the natural order of things. In the southern half of the world, so the system teaches, violence and hunger belong not to history but to nature, and justice and liberty have been condemned to mutual hatred.

FORGETTING/1

I am reading a novel by Louise Erdrich.

At one point, a great grandfather meets his great grandson. The great grandfather is completely senile *("his thoughts are the color of water")* and displays the same beatific smile as his newly born great grandson. The great grandfather is happy because he has lost his memory. His great grandson is happy because he doesn't yet have any memory. This, I imagine, is perfect felicity. I want no part of it.

FORGETTING/2

Fear dries the mouth, moistens the hands and mutilates. Fear of knowing condemns us to ignorance, fear of doing reduces us to impotence. Military dictatorship, fear of listening, fear of speaking, made us deaf and dumb. Now democracy, with its fear of remembering, infects us with amnesia, but you don't have to be Sigmund Freud to know that no carpet can hide the garbage of memory.

FEAR

One morning they gave us a guinea pig. It came to the house in a cage. At midday, I opened the door of the cage.

I returned home at nightfall and found the guinea pig just as I had left it: inside the cage, huddled against the bars, trembling with the fear of freedom.

THE RIVER OF OBLIVION

The first time I went to Galicia, my friends took me to the
River of Oblivion. My friends told me that in the old impe-
rial days, the Roman legionnaires had wanted to invade these
lands but had not passed that point: paralyzed by fear, they
had stopped at this river bank. And they never crossed over,
for whoever crosses the River of Oblivion arrives on the
other side not knowing who he is or where he comes from.

I was beginning my exile in Spain and I thought: If the
waters of a river are enough to erase one's memory, what will
happen to me, the flotsam of a shipwreck, who crossed an
entire ocean? But I had been traveling through the small
towns of Pontevedra and Orense, and had discovered taverns

and cafés bearing names like "Uruguay" or "Venezuela" or
"Mi Buenos Aires Querido," and cantinas offering barbecue
or *arepas,* and the team pennants of Peñarol, National, and
Boca Juniors were everywhere, and all of this was due to the
Galicians who had returned from America and now experi-
enced reverse nostalgia. They had left their villages, exiles
like myself, although the economy had chased them out
rather than the police, and many years later they were back in
their homeland and they had never forgotten a thing. Not
when they left, nor when they were over there, nor when
they returned: they had never forgotten a thing. And now
they had two memories and two countries.

FORGETTING/3

In the French Caribbean islands, history books present Napoleon as the most admirable warrior of the West. In these islands, Napoleon restored slavery in 1802. With fire and sword, he forced the free blacks back into slavery on the plantations. Of this, the texts make no mention. The blacks are Napoleon's grandchildren, not his victims.

FORGETTING/4

Chicago is full of factories. There are even factories right in the center of the city, around the world's tallest building. Chicago is full of factories. Chicago is full of workers.

Arriving in the Haymarket district, I ask my friends to show me the place where the workers whom the whole world salutes every May 1st were hanged in 1886.

"It must be around here," they tell me. But nobody knows where.

No statue has been erected in memory of the martyrs of Chicago in the city of Chicago. Not a statue, not a monolith, not a bronze plaque. Nothing.

May 1st is the only truly universal day of all humanity, the only day when all histories and all geographies, all languages and religions and cultures of the world coincide. But in the

United States, May 1st is a day like any other. On that day, people work normally and no one, or almost no one, remembers that the rights of the working class did not spring whole from the ear of a goat, or from the hand of God or the boss.

After my fruitless exploration of the Haymarket, my friends take me to the largest bookstore in the city. And there, poking around, just by accident, I discover an old poster that seems to be waiting for me, stuck among many movie and rock posters. The poster displays an African proverb: *Until lions have their own historians, histories of the hunt will glorify the hunter.*

CELEBRATION OF SUBJECTIVITY

I had been writing *Memory of Fire* for a long time, and the more I wrote the more I entered into the stories I was telling. I was already having trouble distinguishing past from present: what had happened was happening, happening all around me, and writing was my way of striking out and embracing. However, history books supposedly are not subjective.

I mentioned this to José Coronel Urtecho: in this book I'm writing, however you look at it, backwards or forwards, in the light or against it, my loves and quarrels can be seen at a single glance.

And on the banks of the San Juan River, the old poet told me that there is no fucking reason to pay attention to the fanatics of objectivity:

"Don't worry," he said to me. *"That's how it should be. Those who make objectivity a religion are liars. They are scared of human pain. They don't want to be objective, it's a lie: they want to be objects, so as not to suffer."*

CELEBRATION OF THE
MARRIAGE OF HEART AND MIND

Why does one write, if not to put one's pieces together? From the moment we enter school or church, education chops us into pieces: it teaches us to divorce soul from body and mind from heart. The fishermen of the Colombian coast must be learned doctors of ethics and morality, for they invented the word *sentipensante,* feeling-thinking, to define language that speaks the truth.

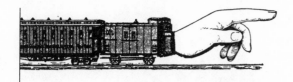

DIVORCES

Our system is one of detachment: to keep silenced people from asking questions, to keep the judged from judging, to keep solitary people from joining together, and the soul from putting together its pieces.

The system divorces feeling from thought as it divorces sex from love, private life from public life, past from present. If the past has nothing to say to the present, history may go on sleeping undisturbed in the closet where the system keeps its old disguises.

The system empties our memory or fills it with garbage, and so it teaches us to repeat history instead of making it. Tragedy repeats itself as farce, the famous prophecy announced. But with us it is worse: tragedy is repeated as tragedy.

CELEBRATION OF
CONTRADICTIONS/1

Idiot memory repeats itself as tragic litany. Lively memory, on the other hand, is born every day, springing from the past and set against it. Of all the words in the German language, *aufheben* was Hegel's favorite. *Aufheben* means both to preserve and to annul, and thus pays homage to human history, which is born as it dies and builds as it destroys.

CELEBRATION OF
CONTRADICTIONS/2

Turn loose the voices, undream the dreams. Through my writing, I try to express the magical reality, which I find at the core of the hideous reality of America.

In these countries, the god Elegguá carries death in the nape of his neck and life in his face. Every promise is a threat, every loss a discovery. Courage is born of fear, certainty of doubt. Dreams announce the possibility of another reality, and out of delirium emerges another kind of reason.

What it all comes down to is that we are the sum of our efforts to change who we are. Identity is no museum piece sitting stock-still in a display case, but rather the endlessly astonishing synthesis of the contradictions of everyday life.

I believe in that fugitive faith. It seems to me the only faith worthy of belief for its great likeness to the human animal, accursed yet holy, and to the mad adventure that is living in this world.

CHRONICLE OF THE CITY
OF MEXICO

Half a century after the appearance of Superman in Gotham City, Superbarrio watches over the streets and rooftops of Mexico City. The prestigious North American Man of Steel, universal symbol of power, lives in a city called Metropolis. Superbarrio, an ordinary flesh and blood Mexican, hero of the common folk, lives in a slum called Nezahualcoyotl.

Superbarrio has a pot belly and bow legs. He wears a red mask and a yellow cape. He does not do battle against mummies, ghosts or vampires. At one end of the city, he confronts the police and saves some starving people from eviction while at the other end, at the same time, he leads a demonstration for women's rights or against the poisoning of the air. Meanwhile, in the center of the city, he invades the National Congress and makes a speech denouncing government foul play.

THE CLASH OF SYMBOLS

Through alchemy or the deviltry of the people, symbols resolve their contradictions and poison is turned into bread.

In Havana, a stone's throw from the Casa de las Américas, stands a singular monument: a pair of bronze shoes atop an enormous pedestal.

The lone pair of shoes belonged to the servile Tomás Estrada Palma. The infuriated people toppled the statue, leaving only its shoes.

At the turn of the century, Estrada Palma had been president of Cuba under its colonial occupation by the United States.

PARADOXES

If contradiction is the lung of history, it seems to me that paradox must be the mirror that history uses to pull our leg.

Not even God's own son saved himself from paradox. He chose to be born in a subtropical desert where it has never snowed, yet snow has become the universal symbol of the Nativity ever since the Europe decided Jesus was a European. And to add insult to INRI, the birth of Jesus is nowadays the business that brings the most money to the money-changers Jesus expelled from the temple.

Napoleon Bonaparte, the most French of Frenchmen, was not French. Joseph Stalin, the most Russian of Russians, was not Russian, and the most German of Germans, Adolf Hitler, was born in Austria. Margharita Sarfatti, the woman most loved by the anti-Semite Mussolini, was Jewish. José Carlos Mariátegui, the most Marxist of Latin American Marxists, fervently believed in God. Che Guevara had been declared *completely unfit for military life* by the Argentine army.

At the hands of a sculptor named Aleijadinho, the ugliest

of Brazilians, Brazil's greatest beauties were born. North American blacks, the most oppressed of peoples, created jazz, the freest of all musics. Don Quixote, the most errant of knights, was conceived in the confines of a prison. And as a final paradox, Don Quixote never uttered his most famous phrase. He never said: *"The dogs are barking, Sancho. Time to saddle up."*

"You look nervous," says the hysteric. *"I hate you,"* says the lover. *"There will be no devaluation,"* says the Minister of the Economy on the eve of devaluation. *"The military respects the constitution,"* says the Minister of Defense on the eve of the coup d'état.

In its war against the Sandinista revolution, the government of the United States coincided paradoxically with the Communist Party of Nicaragua. And when all is said and done, the Sandinista barricades during the Somoza dictatorship were paradoxical: the barricades, which closed the street, cleared the way.

THE SYSTEM/1

Functionaries don't function.
Politicians speak but say nothing.
Voters vote but don't elect.
The information media disinform.
Schools teach ignorance.
Judges punish the victims.
The military makes war against its compatriots.
The police don't fight crime because they are too busy committing it.
Bankruptcies are socialized while profits are privatized.
Money is freer than people are.
People are at the service of things.

IN PRAISE OF COMMON SENSE

Early one morning near the end of 1985, Colombian radio listeners were informed:

"The city of Armero has been wiped off the map."

The neighboring volcano had killed it. No one could out-run the avalanche of boiling mud. A wave as big as the sky and as hot as hell swept over the city, puffing smoke and snorting like a furious, wild beast, swallowing thirty thousand people, houses and all.

The volcano had been sending out warnings for a year. For a year it had been spewing fire and, unable to wait any longer, it bombarded the city with thunder and rained down ashes so that the deaf might hear and the blind might see the many warnings. But the mayor said that the federal government saw no cause for alarm, and the priest said that the bishop said God was taking care of the matter, and the geologists and the vulcanologists said that everything was under control and there was no further risk of danger.

The city of Amero died of civilization. It had not yet celebrated its centennial anniversary. It possessed neither anthem nor coat of arms.

INDIANS / 1

Returning from Temuco, I doze off on the road.

Suddenly, the splendor of the landscape awakens me. The Repocura valley appears and glows before my eyes, as if someone suddenly had drawn back a curtain on another world.

But these lands no longer belong to everyone and to no one, as before. A decree of the Pinochet dictatorship has smashed the communities, forcing the Indians into isolation. They nevertheless insist on putting their poverties together and they still work together, are silent together, and speak together:

"You people have had fifteen years of dictatorship," they explain to my Chilean friends. *"We've had five centuries of it."*

We sit in a circle. We are gathered in a medical center which does not have and never has had a doctor, health worker, nurse, or anything at all.

"One lives to die, and that's that." says one of the women.

The Indians, guilty of being incapable of private property, do not exist.

In Chile, there are no Indians: just Chileans, say government posters.

INDIANS/2

Language as betrayal: They shout *hangman* at them. In Ecuador, the hangmen call their victims hangmen:

"Indian hangman!" they shout.

One out of every three Ecuadorians is an Indian. The other two make the former pay every day for his historical defeat.

"We are the conquered ones. They won the war. We lost by trusting them. That's why," says Miguel, born deep in the Amazon jungle.

They are treated like the blacks in South Africa. Indians may not enter hotels or restaurants.

"At school they beat me when I spoke our language," says Lucho, born in the southern sierra.

"My father forbade me to talk Quechua. 'It's for your own good,' he would tell me," recalled Rosa, Lucho's wife.

Rosa and Lucho live in Quito. They are used to hearing:

"Shitty Indian."

Indians are stupid—vagrants, drunks. But the system that despises them despises what it does not know, because it doesn't know what it fears. Behind the mask of scorn is panic: Those ancient voices, stubbornly alive: What are they saying? What do they say when they speak? What do they say when they are silent?

TRADITIONS OF THE FUTURE

There is just one place where yesterday and today meet, recognize each other, and embrace, and that place is tomorrow.

Certain voices from the American past, long past, sound very futuristic. For example, the ancient voice that still tells us we are children of the earth and that our mother is not for sale or for hire. While dead birds rain on Mexico City and rivers are turned into sewers, oceans into dumps and forests into deserts, this voice, stubbornly refusing to die, heralds another world different from this one that poisons the water, soil, air and soul.

The ancient voice that speaks to us of community heralds another world as well. Community—the communal mode of production and life—is the oldest of American traditions, the most American of all. It belongs to the earliest days and the first people, but it also belongs to the times ahead and anticipates a new New World. For there is nothing less alien to these lands of ours than socialism. Capitalism, on the other hand, is foreign: like smallpox, like the flu, it came from abroad.

THE KINGDOM OF THE COCKROACH

When I visited Cedric Belfrage in Cuernavaca, Los Angeles contained 16 million personmobiles, people with wheels instead of legs, so it did not much resemble the city he had known when he arrived in Hollywood during the silent film era, nor did it resemble the city Cedric still loved when Senator McCarthy expelled him during the witch hunts.

Since his expulsion, Cedric has lived in Cuernavaca. Certain friends, survivors of the old days, turn up from time to time at his roomy and luminous house; and also, from time to time, comes a mysterious white butterfly that drinks tequila.

I was coming from Los Angeles and had been in the area where Cedric had lived, but he did not ask me about Los Angeles. Los Angeles did not interest him, or he acted as if it

didn't. Instead, he asked me about my time in Canada and we got to talking about acid rain. The poisonous gasses from the factories, which the clouds returned to the earth, had already exterminated 14,000 lakes in Canada. Those 14,000 lakes no longer sustained any life: neither plants nor fish. I had had a glimpse of that catastrophe.

Old Cedric looked at me with his big, clear eyes and feigned obeisances to those soon to reign over the earth:

"We human beings have abdicated the planet," he proclaimed, *"in favor of the cockroaches."*

Then he took the bottle and filled our glasses:

"A spot more while we may."

INDIANS/3

Jean-Marie Simon heard about it in Guatemala. It took place at the close of 1983, in the village of Tabil, in southern Quiché.

The army was carrying out its campaign to exterminate all indigenous communities. In less than three years, they had wiped four hundred villages off the map. They were burning crops and killing Indians. They burned crops down to the roots, and killed children. *"We'll leave them without a seed to sow,"* announced Colonel Horacio Maldonado Shadd.

And so, one afternoon they arrived at the village of Tabil.

They dragged five prisoners from their houses, bound hand and foot and badly beaten. All five were natives of the village where they had lived and multiplied; but the officer said they were Cuban agents, enemies of the nation, that the villagers would have to decide how the five should be punished and then carry out the sentence. They were given loaded weapons in case they decided the five should be shot. The colonel told the villagers they had until noon the next day.

The Indians assembled to discuss the situation:

"These men are our brothers. They are innocent. If we don't kill them, the soldiers will kill us."

They talked all night long. The prisoners lay in the middle of the assembly, listening.

Dawn came and the villagers were no further along than when they started. They had reached no decision and were feeling increasingly bewildered.

So they appealed to the gods for assistance: to the Mayan gods and the god of the Christians.

They awaited a response in vain. None of the gods said a thing. They all were mute.

Meanwhile, the soldiers were waiting somewhere in the woods outside of town.

The inhabitants of Tabil watched as the sun rose implacably toward its zenith. The prisoners, on their feet, fell silent.

Shortly before midday, the soldiers heard the shots.

INDIANS/4

On Vancouver Island, Ruth Benedict tells us, the Indians staged tournaments to measure the greatness of their princes. The rivals competed by destroying their belongings. They threw their canoes, fish oil, and salmon eggs on the fire, and from a high promontory, hurled their cloaks and pots into the sea.

Whoever got rid of everything, won.

The Anthropological Society of Paris classified them like insects: the skin color of the Huitoto Indians measured 29 to 30 on its chromatic scale.

The Peruvian Amazon Company hunted them down like beasts. The slave labor of the Huitoto supplied the world market with rubber. When the company caught an Indian who had fled the plantations, he was wrapped in a Peruvian flag soaked in kerosene, and burned alive.

Michael Taussig has studied the culture of terror that capitalist civilization sowed in the Amazon jungle in the first years of the twentieth century. Torture was not used to gather information, but as a ceremonial reaffirmation of power. In a long and solemn ritual, they would cut out the Indian's tongue and *then* torture him to make him speak.

Extortion,
insults,
threats,
slapping,
beating,
thrashing,
whipping,
the dark room,
the icy shower,
enforced fasting,
forced feeding,
the ban on leaving the house,
the ban on saying what you think,
the ban on doing what you feel,
and public humiliation
are some of the methods of punishment and torture traditional to family life. To punish disobedience and discipline liberty, family tradition perpetuates a culture of terror that humiliates women, teaches children to lie, and spreads the plague of fear.

"Human rights should begin at home," Andrés Dominguez told me in Chile.

THE CULTURE OF TERROR/3

Concerning the model child:

A little girl playing with two dolls chides them to be still. She seems like a doll herself, so pretty and good and not bothering anyone.

(From the book *Adelante* by J. H. Figueira, a textbook used in Uruguayan schools until very recently.)

In a parochial school in Seville, a child of nine or ten was confessing his sins for the first time. The child confessed that he had stolen candy, or had lied to his mother, or had copied from the pupil next to him, or perhaps he confessed that he had masturbated thinking about his cousin. Then, from the darkness of the confessional, the priest's hand emerged, brandishing a bronze cross. The priest forced the child to kiss the crucified Jesus and hitting him on the mouth with the cross, said:

"You killed him, you killed him. . . ."

Julio Vélez was that kneeling Andalusian child. Many years have passed. He has never been able to root it from his memory.

Ramóna Caraballo was given away as a present when she could hardly walk.

Back in 1950, when still a child, she was a little slave in a home in Montevideo. She did everything in exchange for nothing.

One day, her grandmother came to visit her. Ramona did not know her or remember her. Her grandmother came from the country, in a state because she had to get back to her village at once. She came in, gave her granddaughter a terrible thrashing, and departed.

She left Ramona weeping and bleeding.

Her grandmother had told her as she raised the whip:

"I'm not beating you for what you have done. I'm beating you for what you're going to do."

THE CULTURE OF TERROR/6

Pedro Algorta, a lawyer, showed me the fat dossier about the murder of two women. The double crime had been committed with a knife at the end of 1982, in a Montevideo suburb.

The accused, Alma Di Agosto, had confessed. She had been in jail more than a year, and she was apparently condemned to rot there for the rest of her life.

As is the custom, the police had raped and tortured her. After a month of continuous beatings they had extracted several confessions. Alma Di Agosto's confessions did not much resemble each other, as if she had committed the same murder in many different ways. Different people appeared in each confession, picturesque phantoms without names or addresses, because the electric cattle prod turns anyone into a prolific storyteller. Furthermore, the author demonstrated the

agility of an Olympic athlete, the strength of a fairground Amazon, and the dexterity of a professional matador. But most surprising was the wealth of detail: in each confession, the accused described with millimetric precision clothing, gestures, surroundings, positions, objects. . . .

Alma Di Agosto was blind.

Her neighbors, who knew and loved her, were convinced she was guilty:

"Why?" asked the lawyer.

"Because the papers say so."

"But the papers lie," said the lawyer.

"But the radio says so too," explained the neighbors. *"And the TV!"*

TELEVISION/1

It was a fleapit on the outskirts of the city, the cheapest there was in Santa Fe and in the whole of the Argentine republic: a wretched shack that was falling to pieces before they even put it up, but Fernando Birri never missed any of the films or ceremonies presented in the darkness of this pretentious temple of his childhood.

In this movie theater, the Cine Doré, Fernando once saw several episodes concerning the mysteries of ancient Egypt. There was a pharaoh, seated on his throne before a reflecting pool. The pharaoh seemed to be asleep but he was running a finger through his beard. As he did so, he opened his eyes and made a signal. Then the royal magician pronounced a spell and the waters of the pool grew agitated and caught fire. When the flames were doused and the waters quieted, the pharaoh leaned out over the pool. There, in the limpid water, he saw all that was happening at that moment in Egypt and the world.

Half a century later, recollecting the pharaoh of his childhood, Fernando was sure of one thing: that magic pool in which could be seen all that was happening far away was a television.

TELEVISION/2

Does television show what happens?

In our countries, television shows what it would like to happen, and nothing happens if it is not shown on television.

Television, that final light that saves you from loneliness and from the night, *is* reality. Because life is a show, the system promises those who behave themselves a comfortable seat.

SHOWBIZ CULTURE

Offscreen, the world is a shadow unworthy of confidence.

Before television, before the movies, it was already so. When Buffalo Bill seized some unsuspecting Indian and managed to kill him, he immediately proceeded to tear off his hairy scalp, feathers, and other trophies, and in a single gallop hurtled from the Wild West to the theaters of New York, where he repeated the heroic deed he had just performed. Then, as the curtain rose and Buffalo Bill raised his bloody knife onstage, reality occurred for the very first time there in the footlights.

TELEVISION/3

The TV hurls out images that reproduce the system and voices that echo it, and there is no spot on earth it does not reach. The entire planet is a huge suburb of Dallas. We eat imported emotions as if they were canned sausages while the young children of television, trained to watch life instead of making it, shrug their shoulders.

In Latin America, freedom of expression consists of the right to protest on a few radio stations and in local newspapers. It has become unnecessary for the police to ban books: their price alone bans them.

THE DIGNITY OF ART

I write for those who cannot read me: the downtrodden, the ones who have been waiting on line for centuries to get into history, who cannot read a book or afford to buy one.

When I begin to lose heart, it does me good to recall a lesson in the dignity of art which I learned years ago at a theater in Assisi, in Italy. Helena and I had gone to see an evening of pantomime and no one else showed up. The two of us made up the entire audience. When the lights dimmed, we were joined by the usher and the ticket seller. Yet despite the fact that there were more people on stage than in the audience, the actors worked as hard as if they were basking in the glory of a full house on opening night. They put their hearts and souls into the performance and it was marvelous.

Our applause shook the empty hall. We clapped until our hands were sore.

TELEVISION/4

I was told this by Rosa María Mateo, one of Spain's most popular television entertainers. A woman had written her a letter from some remote village asking her please to tell her the truth:

"When I look at you, do you look at me?"

Rosa María told me this and said that she didn't know how to respond.

TELEVISION/5

In the summer, Uruguayan television presents long programs about Punta del Este. More interested in things than in people, the cameras go into ecstasy as they show the houses of the vacationing rich. These ostentatious mansions resemble the marble and bronze mausoleums of La Recoleta cemetery, the Punta del Este of the hereafter.

Across the screen parade the elect and their symbols of power. The system, which builds the social pyramid from the top down, rewards few people. Here are the prize winners: well-manicured usurers, merchants of expensive teeth, politicians with growing noses and doctors with rubber spines.

Television sets out to worship those who command in the River Plate basin, but performs an exemplary didactic function without even intending to do so: it takes us to the social heights and reveals the vacuousness and bad taste of the triumphant money hunters.

Beneath the superficial stupidity is real stupidity.

CELEBRATION OF MISTRUST

On the first day of classes, the professor brought out an enormous flask.

"It's full of perfume," he told Miguel Brun and the rest of the students. *"I want to measure how perceptive each one of you is. Raise your hand as soon as you perceive the scent."*

And he removed the stopper. Moments later two hands were in the air. Soon five, ten, thirty—all hands were raised.

"May I open the window, professor?" a young woman asked, dizzy from the overpowering fragrance. Several voices echoed her request. The air, thick with the aroma of perfume, had quickly become unbearable for everyone.

Then the professor had the students examine the flask, one by one. It was full of water.

THE CULTURE OF TERROR/7

Blatant colonialism mutilates you without pretense: it forbids you to talk, it forbids you to act, it forbids you to exist. Invisible colonialism, however, convinces you that serfdom is your destiny and impotence is your nature: it convinces you that it's *not possible* to speak, *not possible* to act, *not possible* to exist.

ALIENATION/1

Back in my salad days, I was a bank clerk.

Among the customers, I recall a shirt manufacturer. The manager of the bank would renew his loans purely out of pity. The poor shirtmaker was constantly on the brink of bankruptcy. His shirts were not bad, but no one bought them.

One night, the shirtmaker was visited by an angel. When he woke that morning he had seen the light. He sprang out of bed.

The first thing he did was to change the name of his enterprise to Uruguay Sociedad Anónima, a patriotic name whose initials are: U.S.A. The second thing he did was to sew labels onto the collars of his shirts that said, with complete honesty: *Made in U.S.A.* The third thing he did was to sell shirts like hotcakes. And the fourth was to pay off his debts and make tons of money.

ALIENATION/2

Those in power believe that he is best who copies best. Official culture extols the virtues of the monkey and the parrot. Alienation in Latin America: a circus show. Importation, imposition: our cities are full of triumphal arches, obelisks and parthenons. Bolivia has no ocean, but it has admirals done up like Lord Nelson. Lima has no rain, but it has peaked roofs with gutters. In Managua, one of the hottest cities in the world, condemned to a perpetual rolling boil, there are mansions flaunting magnificent fireplaces, and at Somoza's parties, society ladies sported silver fox stoles.

ALIENATION/3

Alastair Reid writes for the *New Yorker* but rarely goes to New York.

He prefers to live on a remote beach in the Dominican Republic. Christopher Columbus landed on this beach several centuries ago on one of his excursions to Japan, and nothing has changed since.

From time to time, the postman appears among the trees. The postman arrives staggering under his load. Alastair receives mountains of correspondence. From the U.S., he is bombarded with commercial offers, leaflets, catalogues, luxurious temptations from the consumer civilization that exhorts him to buy.

On one occasion, he found in the mass of paper an advertisement for a rowing machine. Alastair showed it to his neighbors, the fishermen.

"Indoors? They use it indoors?"

The fishermen couldn't believe it:

"*Without water? They row without water?*"

They couldn't believe it, they couldn't comprehend it:

"*And without fish? And without the sun? And without the sky?*"

The fishermen told Alastair that they got up every night long before dawn and put out to sea and cast their nets as the sun rose over the horizon, and that this was their life and that this life pleased them, but that rowing was the one infernal aspect of the whole business:

"*Rowing is the one thing we hate,*" said the fishermen.

Then Alastair explained to them that the rowing machine was for exercise.

"*For what?*"

"*Exercise.*"

"*Ah. And exercise—what's that?*"

EDUARDO GALEANO

THE WALLS SPEAK/3

In Montevideo, in the neighborhood of Brazo Oriental:

Here we sit, watching them kill our dreams.

And on the breakwater facing the Montevidean port of Buceo:

Old fart: you can't live your whole life in fear.

In red letters along an entire block on Colón Avenue in Quito:

What if we got together and gave that big gray bubble a kick?

NAMES / 1

People, creatures and things trooped to the house of names looking to call themselves something. The names jingled as they offered themselves: they promised to sound good and to have resonant echoes. The house was always full of people and animals and things trying on names. Helena dreamed of the house of names and discovered there the puppy Pepa Lumpen, who was looking for a more presentable name.

NAMES/2

Arturo Alape tells me that Manuel Marulanda Vélez was not the real name of that famous Colombian guerrilla. Forty years ago, when he became a rebel, his name was Pedro Antonio Marín. In those days, Marulanda was someone else: dark skinned, huge, a bricklayer by trade, and left-handed in his way of thinking. When the police beat Marulanda to death, his comrades got together and decided that Marulanda could not be allowed to die. They unanimously gave the name to Marín, who has used it ever since.

The Mexican, Pancho Villa, also bore the name of a friend murdered by the police.

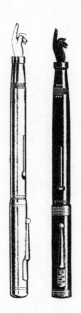

NAMES/3

Since I began to write, I have signed my name Galeano, which is my maternal surname. This occurred when I was nineteen, or perhaps only a few days old, for calling myself that was a way of being born again.

Previously, when I was a kid and was publishing drawings, I signed them Gius, because my paternal surname was difficult to pronounce in Spanish. (I got the name Hughes from my Welsh great grandfather, who went to sea at fifteen from the port of Liverpool and made it to the Caribbean, Santo Domingo, and some time later, Río de Janeiro, then finally Montevideo. There he threw his Mason's ring into the Miguelete River and put up the first barbed wire in the fields of Paysandú, making himself master of land and people. He died a century ago while translating *Martín Fierro* into English.)

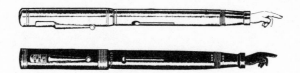

Over the years, I have heard conflicting versions of this business about my chosen name. The version that most offends the intelligence attributes to me anti-imperialist intentions. The most comical version imputes motives of conspiracy or smuggling. And the most screwed-up version makes me the red sheep of my family: it invents for me a hostile and oligarchic father instead of the actual father I have, a fabulous guy who always earned his living by his own work or good luck in the soccer pools.

The Japanese painter Hokusai changed his name sixty times, to celebrate each of his sixty births. In Uruguay, a formal country, they would have locked him up as a madman or a perfidious forger of false identities.

BACK TO THE FUTURE

At the beginning of the twentieth century, Uruguay was a
twenty-first–century country. Now, at the end of the twentieth century, Uruguay belongs to the nineteenth.

In the land of boredom, etiquette prohibits all that routine
does not impose. Men dream of retirement, and women of
marriage. Youngsters, guilty of the crime of youth, are sentenced to solitary confinement or driven into exile unless and
until they can prove they are old.

DAZED DAYS

My certainties breakfast on doubts. And there are days when I feel like a stranger in Montevideo and anywhere else. On those days, days without sunshine, moonless nights, no place is my own and I do not recognize myself in anything or anyone. Words do not resemble what they refer to or even correspond to their own sounds. Then I am not where I am. I leave my body and travel far, heading nowhere, and I do not want to be with anybody, not even with myself, and I have no name nor wish to have any: then I lose all desire to call myself or be called.

WHEN LUCK RUNS OUT

During streaks of bad luck, I lose everything. Things fall out of my pockets and my memory: I lose keys, pens, money, documents, names, faces, words. I don't know whether someone wishes me harm and has put the evil eye on me or whether it's pure happenstance, but sometimes this slump just won't end and I lose one thing after another. I lose what I find, I can't find what I'm looking for, and I'm quite afraid of losing life through some little hole in my pocket.

ONETTI

I was not yet twenty and still playing blind man's bluff in the nights of the world.

I wanted to paint and couldn't. I wanted to write and didn't know how. From time to time, I would write some story and on occasion, I would take it to Juan Carlos Onetti.

He was always lying in bed, out of laziness, out of sadness, surrounded by pyramids of cigarette butts, behind a wall of empty bottles. I felt obliged to spout superintelligent phrases. Maestro Onetti stared at the ceiling and didn't open his mouth except to yawn, smoke and drink—languid drowsiness, languid puffing, languid drinking—and perhaps mumble some conclusion reached after long meditation on the national and international scene.

"It all got fucked up," he said, *"the day the military and the women learned to read."*

Seated at his side, I would wait for him to tell me that those stories of mine were undoubtedly the work of genius, but he would say nothing, finally grunting out words of encouragement like:

"Look, kid. If Beethoven had been born in Tacuarembó, he would have ended up conducting the local band."

ARGUEDAS

I was returning to Montevideo at the end of a trip. I don't remember where I was coming from, but I do remember that on the plane I read *The Fox Above and the Fox Below*, José María Arguedas' last novel. Arguedas had begun writing this farewell to life the day he decided to kill himself, and the novel was his long and desperate testament. I read the book and believed him: from the very first page, I believed him. Although I had never met the man, I believed him as if he were my old friend.

In *The Fox*, Arguedas had dedicated to Onetti the highest praise one writer could bestow on another: he had written that although he was in Santiago de Chile, he truly wished he were in Montevideo, *to meet Onetti and shake the hand with which he writes.*

In Onetti's house, I mentioned this. He hadn't known. The novel, just published, still hadn't reached Montevideo. I mentioned it to Onetti and he didn't say a word. Only a short while earlier, Arguedas had blown his head apart.

A long time—minutes or years—passed while the two of us sat there in silence. Then I said something, asked something, and Onetti didn't respond. I looked up and I saw the moisture running down his face.

CELEBRATION OF SILENCE/1

It had been years since I last saw Fernando Rodríguez. The winds of exile, which separate so much, brought us together. I found him, as usual, tattered and grumpy.

"You haven't changed a bit," I told him.

He told me he had a few years left but not many:

"One shouldn't live beyond the age of eighty because then one develops vices and doesn't want to die."

That night we let ourselves wander aimlessly, between the sea and the train tracks in Calella de la Costa. We walked slowly, both of us silent, and around the corner from the station we sat down to have some coffee. Then Fernando said something about the dungeon where the military had put Raúl Sendic, the Tupamaro, and together we called forth memories of Raúl and his way of life. Fernando asked me:

"Did you read what the papers said when they got him?"

The newspapers reported that he had emerged from his hiding place, gun in hand, opening fire and yelling: "I am Rufo and I'm not surrendering."

"Yes," I said, *"I read it."*

"Ah. And did you believe it?"

"No."

"I didn't either," said Fernando. *"That guy would give in quietly."*

CELEBRATION OF SILENCE/2

The singer Braulio López, half of the duo Los Olimareños, arrived in Barcelona as an exile. One of his hands was broken.

Braulio had been a prisoner in the Villa Dovoto jail for possessing three books: a biography of José Artigas, some poems by Antonio Machado, and Saint-Exupéry's *The Little Prince*. When they were about to release him, a jailer had come into his cell and asked: *"You the guitar player?"* And then he stepped on Braulio's left hand with his boot.

I suggested that I interview him. The story might interest the magazine *Triunfo*. But Braulio scratched his head, thought for a moment, then said:

"No."

And he explained to me:

"My hand will heal, sooner or later. Then I'll be playing and singing again. See? I don't want to doubt the applause."

CELEBRATION OF
THE HUMAN VOICE/4

Manfred Max-Neef, who lived in Uruguay over twenty years ago, told me what he most remembered: *"The dogs barked sitting down and the people kept their word."*

Then the military dictatorship restored order, forcing Uruguayans to lie or be silent. I don't know if the dogs then stood up to bark, but to keep your word was to keep nothing at all.

THE SYSTEM/2

It's the age of the chameleon: no one has taught humanity so much as that humble little creature.

Experts in concealment are highly respected, homage is paid to the culture of the mask. We speak the double language of master mimics. Double language, double accounting, double morality: one morality for speech, another morality for action. The morality for action is called realism.

The law of reality is the law of power. So that reality should not seem unreal, those in charge tell us that morality must be immoral.

CELEBRATION OF THE MARRIAGE OF WORD AND DEED

I read an article by a playwright, Arkady Raikin, published in a Moscow magazine. Bureaucracy, says the writer, sees to it that action, words and thoughts never meet. Action stays at the workplace, words in meetings, and thoughts on the pillow.

A considerable part of the power of Che Guevara, I think, that mysterious energy that far outlives his death and his errors, comes from a very simple fact: he was that rare kind of person who says what he thinks and does what he says.

THE SYSTEM/3

If you're not quick, you're dead. You are obliged to be the screwer or the screwed, the liar or the target of lies. These are times of what do I care, what can you do about it, don't interfere, look out for number one. A time of swindlers: production yields nothing, creation is pointless, work has no value.

In the River Plate basin, we call the heart a *bobo,* a fool. And not because it falls in love: we call it a fool because it works.

IN PRAISE OF
PRIVATE INITIATIVE

*J*esus is watching you. Wherever you go, His eyes follow.

Modern technology helps the Son of God do His job of policing the universe. Three sheets of polarized plastic successively blocking the passage of light assist Him in this task.

In 1961 or 1962, one of those shifty-eyed pictures caught a reporter's attention. Julio Tacovilla was walking along some street in Buenos Aires when he felt himself observed. From a store window, Jesus had riveted His eyes on Julio. Julio took a step backward and the eyes followed him backward. He stood still and the eyes stayed with him. He walked forward and the eyes followed.

This divine sign changed his life and lifted him out of poverty.

Soon afterward, Tacovilla flew to Port-au-Prince, and through the Argentine embassy in Haiti arranged an audience with the president-for-life, "Papa Doc" Duvalier.

Under his arm was a large picture.

"I would like to show you something, Your Excellency," he said.

It was a portrait of the dictator. Its eyes moved.

"Papa Doc is watching you," Tacovilla explained.

Papa Doc nodded his head.

"Not bad," he said, walking back and forth in front of the portrait. *"How many can you make?"*

"How much can you spend?"

"Whatever it costs."

And thus Haiti was filled with vigilant eyes and the enterprising reporter's pockets were filled with money.

THE PERFECT CRIME

This is the way things work in London: the radiators give out heat in exchange for the coins they receive. And in midwinter, several Latin American exiles were shivering in the cold, without a single coin for the heater in their flat.

They stared without blinking at the radiator. They looked like devotees worshiping before a totem, but they were poor shipwrecked sailors considering how to finish off the British Empire. If they put in coins of tin or cardboard, the radiator would work, but later on the collector would find the evidence of their infamy.

What to do? they asked themselves. The cold was making them tremble as if they had malaria. All at once one of them let out a savage cry that shook the foundations of Western civilization. And so the ice coin was born, invented by a poor frozen man.

They got to work right away. They made wax molds that perfectly reproduced British coins, then they filled the molds with water and put them in the freezer.

The ice coins left no trace because the heat evaporated them.

And thus, that London flat was turned into a Caribbean beach.

EXILE

The military dictatorship had denied me a passport, as it had many Uruguayans, and I was sentenced for life to unravel red tape in the Foreign Section of the Barcelona police station.

Profession? *Writer of forms,* I wrote.

One day, I couldn't take it any longer. I was sick and tired of waiting on lines for hours in the street and fed up with the bureaucrats whom I could no longer bear to face.

"This form is no good."

"I got it here."

"When?"

"Last week."

"There are new forms now."

"May I have some?"

"I don't have any."

"So where can I get them?"

"I don't know. Next."

And then I would need certain stamps, and none of the

windows would have the ones I needed, and I had brought
two photos and needed three, and the machine that took
photos only accepted twenty-five centavo coins and not one
twenty-five peseta coin could be found that day anywhere in
the city of Barcelona.

It was already getting dark when I finally caught the train
to my house in Calella de la Costa. I had been through the
wringer. I fell asleep the instant I sat down.

I was awakened by someone tapping on my shoulder.
Opening my eyes, I saw an outlandish fellow in tattered
pajamas standing over me.

"Passports! . . ."

The madman had torn apart a filthy sheet of newspaper
and was going from car to car, handing out pieces to the
passengers:

"Passports! Have a passport! . . ."

CONSUMER CIVILIZATION

Sometimes, at the end of the summer when the tourists left Calella, you could hear howls coming from the forest. They were the cries of dogs tethered to the trees.

The tourists used the dogs to relieve their loneliness during their vacation, and then, when the time came to leave, tied them up deep in the woods to keep them from following.

CHRONICLE OF THE CITY
OF BUENOS AIRES

In the middle of 1984, I traveled to the River Plate. It was eleven years since I'd seen Montevideo; eight years since I'd seen Buenos Aires. I had walked out of Montevideo because I don't like being a prisoner, and out of Buenos Aires because I don't like being dead. By 1984, the Argentine military dictatorship had gone, leaving behind it an indelible trace of blood and filth, and the Uruguayan military dictatorship was on its way out.

I had just arrived in Buenos Aires. I had not notified my friends. I wanted the reunions to occur spontaneously.

A journalist from Dutch television who had accompanied me on the trip was interviewing me in front of the door of what had been my house. The journalist asked me what had happened to a picture that I used to have hanging in my house, a picture of a harbor, a Montividean port for arriving and not for leaving, a harbor for saying hello and not goodbye, and I began to answer him with my eyes fixed on the red eye of his camera. I told him I did not know where that

picture had ended up, or where its painter, my Uruguayan friend Emilio, the black Emilio Casablanca, had ended up. I had lost the picture and Emilio in the fog as I had many other people and things from those years of terror and loneliness.

As I spoke, I noticed a shadow that passed behind the camera and stood to one side, waiting. When I had finished and the camera's red eye went out, I moved my head and saw him. In that city of 13 million inhabitants, black Emilio had arrived on the corner by pure chance, or whatever it is called, and was in that particular place at that particular moment. We embraced and danced around, and after much embracing, Emilio told me that two weeks ago he had started dreaming that I came back, night after night, and now he couldn't believe it.

And he didn't believe it. That night he called me on the telephone at the hotel to ask if I wasn't a dream or a hallucination, to ask me if I was I.

HOMINGS / 1

In Buenos Aires, I looked for my old café and couldn't find it. I looked for the restaurant where I used to eat enormous platters of *caracú* at all hours of the day or night, and it wasn't there either. Where my favorite pub, the Bachín, had stood, was a mountain of rubble. They had torn down the Bachín, and with it had killed the market where I always would go to buy fruit and flowers or just to partake of that feast for the nose and the eyes. Somebody told me the Bachín had moved and that it was now located somewhere else under another name.

I went there one night. I stood outside the door to this new Bachín that no longer called itself by that name, unsure, yes or no, wondering whether it would constitute betrayal to go in, when a sudden explosion occurred just as I opened the door: the fuses blew and everything was thrown into darkness. I turned around and walked slowly away.

And so I walked for a while, aching with forgotten memories, searching for places and people I didn't find or didn't

know how to find, and finally I crossed the river, the river-sea, and entered Uruguay.

The Uruguayan generals were still in power, but on their way out. It was almost goodbye to the time of terror. I entered, crossing my fingers, and I was lucky.

And walking the streets of the city where I was born, I began to recognize it and felt I was returning without ever having left: Montevideo, sleeping its eternal siesta on the sloping hills of the coast, indifferent to the wind that beats on it and calls to it; Montevideo, boring and beloved, smelling of bread in the summer and smoke in the winter. And I knew I had been longing for home and that the hour for ending my exile had struck. After wandering through many seas, the salmon swims in search of its river, finds it and swims back up it, guided by the smell of the water to the stream where it comes from.

Then, when I returned to Calella to say goodbye, goodbye to Spain, goodbye and thanks, I had a heart attack.

HOMINGS/2

When the drought comes and drains the water from the Uruguay River, the people from Pueblo Federación return to their lost home. As the waters subside, they lay bare a lunar landscape, and the people return.

They now live in a place that is also called Pueblo Federación, the name of the old pueblo before it was drowned beneath the waters, flooded by the Salto Grande dam. No trace of the old pueblo can be seen any longer, not even the cross on the church steeple, and the new pueblo is much more convenient and much prettier. But they return to the old pueblo which the drought gives back to them for as long as it lasts.

They return and inhabit the houses that were their homes and are now war ruins. There, where grandmother died and the first goal and the first kiss took place, they build the fire for the *mate* and the roast, while the dogs scratch at the ground searching for bones they had buried.

TIME

The other evening, Alejandra Adoum tells me, Alina's mother was getting ready to go out. Alina looked at her as, seated before the mirror, she put on her lipstick, traced her eyebrows and powdered her face. She tried on one dress, then another, put on a black coral necklace and a comb in her hair, and her whole body radiated clean and perfumed light. Alina could not take her eyes off her.

"How I'd like to be your age," said Alina.

"I, on the other hand, would give anything to be four years old like you."

That night, when she returned, the mother found Alina awake. Alina hugged her tightly around the legs.

"I feel awful for you," she said sobbing.

RESURRECTIONS/1

Acute myocardial infarct, death clawing at the center of my chest. I spent two weeks sunk in a hospital bed in Barcelona. Then I sacrificed my tattered Porky 2 address book, which was falling apart, and although I could not help it, as I changed address books, I relived the years since the sacrifice of Porky 1. While I was transferring names, addresses and telephone numbers to the new book, I was also getting a clear perspective on the muddle of times and people I had been living with, a whirlwind of many deep joys and sorrows, and this was a prolonged mourning for the dead who had remained in the dead zone of my heart, and a long, much longer celebration of those still alive who fired my blood and swelled my surviving heart. And there was nothing bad and nothing odd about the fact that my heart had broken from so much use.

THE HOUSE

1984 had been a shitty year. Before my heart attack, I had had a back operation and Helena had lost a child halfway to term. When Helena lost the child, the rosebush on the terrace shriveled up. The other flowers died one after another—all of them—though we watered them daily.

The house seemed accursed. And yet, Nani and Alfredo Ahuerma had stayed there for a few days and before leaving, wrote on the mirror:

We were happy in this house.

And we too had found happiness in that house now afflicted with bad luck, and our happiness had managed to conquer uncertainty and bad memories. That sad house, that cheap, ugly house located in a cheap, ugly neighborhood, was a holy place.

1984

THE LOSS

Helena dreamed she was an infant again and couldn't see anything. Groping in the darkness, she cried out for help, for light, but no one turned on the lights. It was pitch black and she could not find her belongings, which were scattered throughout the house and throughout the city, and she sought her things on hands and knees in the darkness and was also looking for cotton or rags or anything at all, because torrents of blood were pouring from between her legs, more and more blood, and although she could see nothing, she felt this thick red river flowing from her body and disappearing in the darkness.

THE EXORCISM

Rosario, the Andalusian witch, had been fighting devils for years. The worst of her demons had been her father-in-law. This wicked fellow had died in bed the night he exclaimed: *"I shit on God,"* and the bronze crucifix fell off the wall and split his skull.

Rosario offered to exorcise our devils. She threw our beautiful Mexican mask of Lucifer in the garbage and censed the house with smoke of rue, marjoram and blessed laurel. Then she knocked a horseshoe into the door with the ends pointing down, hung up some cloves of garlic and scattered about handfuls of salt and plenty of faith.

"Good cheer for hard times and a strum on the guitar for hunger," she said.

Then she said it was up to us, because fate won't help you unless you help it.

FAREWELLS

We had been nine years on the Catalan coast and were about to leave. We only had two or three days left of exile when we awoke to find the beach covered with snow. The sun lit up the snow and set a big white fire ablaze at the edge of the ocean that brought tears to my eyes.

It snowed very rarely on the beach. I had never seen it happen, and there was only one old neighbor from the village who remembered anything like it from days long past.

The ocean looked very happy, licking this enormous plate of ice cream, and my last images of Calella de la Costa were the sea's joy and that radiant field of white.

I wanted to respond to such a beautiful farewell, but nothing occurred to me. Nothing to do, nothing to say. I have never been good at saying goodbye.

DREAMS AT THE END OF EXILE/1

Helena dreamed she was trying to close her suitcase and couldn't, and she pushed down on it with both hands and knelt on it and sat on top of it and stood on top of it, and it wouldn't budge. Mysteries and belongings gushed from the suitcase that wouldn't close.

DREAMS AT THE END OF EXILE/2

Helena was returning to Buenos Aires, but didn't know what language to speak or what currency to use. Standing on the corner of Pueyrredón and Las Heras, she waited for the number 60, which didn't arrive—which never would arrive.

DREAMS AT THE END OF EXILE/3

Her glasses were smashed and her keys were missing. She scoured the city for her keys, groping on hands and knees, and when at last she found them, the keys told her that they didn't open any of her doors.

ROAMINGS/1

Alberto, Helena's father, woke up suddenly. His stomach was splitting with pain. It was the middle of the night and he hadn't eaten any heavy food. Meanwhile, far away, Helena was giving birth to Mariana, The Little Flea.

Years later, Helena's mouth dried out and she found cold sores on her lips while her father battled a fever that nearly killed him. She spoke with his deliriousness although she was in Montevideo and he was in Buenos Aires, and she knew nothing of what was happening. And at the same time, across the sea in a house outside Barcelona, Pilar, one of Helena's friends, woke up bewildered by an inexplicable pounding in her head and said, not knowing why, but with absolute certainty:

"Something is wrong with Helena. Something is wrong."

ROAMINGS/2

This was no stray gust of wind, the kind that wanders aimlessly, but rather a royal gale undoubtedly flung over mountains and national borders from the distant, steamy coast to the city of Medellín. The wind came to Jenny's house and whipped right through it: the front door was suddenly flung open as if a drunk had given it a kick, and a second later, the back door swung open just as violently.

Then Jenny knew. When all was calm again, she even wondered about the wind, the wounded wind, but she knew. And the woman who washed her clothes, who lived far away in the town of La Pintada, also knew: she had been rinsing clothes in rain water at midnight that same night when she heard someone behind her:

"I just saw it, girl. I swear to you."

Early in the morning a telegram arrived in Medellín with the news, already superfluous: at midnight that night, Paula López, Jenny's mother, the washerwoman's dear friend, had died in the distant city of Guayaquil.

CALDWELL'S LAST BEER

It was a Sunday evening in April. After a week of hard work, I was drinking beer in a pub in Amsterdam. I was with Annelies, who had helped me with saintly patience as I traveled around Holland.

I was feeling well and yet, I don't know why, a bit sad. And I started to talk about Erskine Caldwell's novels.

It all began with a dumb joke. Embarrassed by my constant trips to the bathroom between beers, I blurted out that the beer road leads to the bathroom as surely as tobacco road leads to the ashtray, and I thought I was being very witty. But Annelies, who had not read *Tobacco Road*, did not even smile. So I explained the joke to her, which is the worst thing one can do in such a situation, and that was how I got to talking about Caldwell and his horrors of the United States' South. There was no holding me back.

It had been twenty years since I last talked about him. I had not talked about Caldwell since the times when I hung out with Horatio Petit in the cafés and bars of Montevideo, drinking wine and novels.

Now, as I spoke, as the unstoppable torrent gushed from my mouth, I could see Caldwell. I saw him in the shadow of his frayed straw hat, rocking on the verandah, happy about the attacks by the morality leagues and the literary critics, chewing tobacco and dreaming up new idiocies and misadventures for his miserable characters.

Evening turned to night. I don't know how long I spent talking of Caldwell and drinking beer.

The next morning, I read the news in the papers: The novelist Erskine Caldwell died yesterday in his home in the South of the United States.

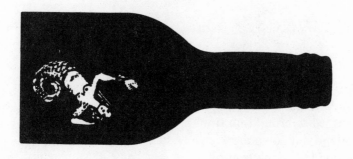

ROAMINGS/3

Helena dreamed that she was talking on the telephone to Pilar and Antonio, and she so wanted to embrace them that she managed to bring them from Spain over the wire. Pilar and Antonio slid down the telephone line as if down a toboggan run and landed, quite unruffled, in our house in Montevideo.

THE WALLS SPEAK/4

Right in the center of Medellín:
No pain, no gain.
And it was signed below:
The killer coach.
In the Uruguayan city of Melo:
Assist the police: torture yourself.
On a wall in Masatepe, Nicaragua, shortly after the fall of
the dictator Somoza:
Though they die of nostalgia, they'll never return.

JEALOUSY FROM ON HIGH

The Maya believe that at the beginning of history, when the gods gave us birth, we humans could see beyond the horizon. We were newly established then, and the gods flung dust in our eyes so we would not be so powerful.

I thought of this jealousy of the gods when I learned of the death of my friend, René Zavaleta. René, who possessed a dazzling intelligence, was struck down by cancer of the brain.

Half a century earlier, Enrico Caruso had died of cancer of the throat.

NEWS

The monkeys are mistaking Felix the Cat for Tarzan, Popeye is devouring his infallible cans, Berta Singerman groans out her poems in the Solis Theater, Geniol's long scissors snip your cold at its root, Mussolini is poised to invade Ethiopia, the British fleet is concentrating around the Suez Canal.

Page after page, day after day in the National Library, the year 1935 parades before Pepe Barriento's eyes. Pepe is searching through back issues of the newspaper *Uruguay* for some news item—the first performance of a tango or the naming of a street or something of the sort, and all the time he feels that this isn't the first time, that what he is seeing now he has seen before, that he has passed this way before, that this is not the first time he has flipped through these pages. The Ariel Cinema has the first run of a Ginger Rogers film, little Shirley Temple is singing and dancing at the Artigas, flannel soaked in Untisal will cure your sore throat, a ship is burning one hundred and fifty miles off the coast of Montevideo, a dancer of dubious reputation is found murdered at dawn, Mussolini pronounces his ultimatum. An enormous headline cries WAR! WAR IS COMING! Yes, Pepe has seen this before. Yes, indeed: that photo, the spread-eagled goalie leaping across the page, the tremendous kick by Cea the Basque, his arms flung out behind him, those headlines: perhaps in his childhood, he thinks. He is surprised to remember a time so far back: in

1935, more than half a century ago, he was six. Then suddenly, he is afraid. Fear's icy fingers scratch the nape of his neck and he knows that he ought to go and knows he will stay.

So he goes on. He could switch newspapers or years, or could simply start to walk toward the door, but he goes on. Pepe goes on, driven; he cannot tear himself away, he cannot stop, and Gestido leads the Peñarol soccer team to victory, and peace has now been signed between Paraguay and Bolivia but the problem remains of what to do with the prisoners, and a storm sinks boats in the English Channel, and the murderer of the dancer has been caught, he turns out to be her lover, eight cents in his pocket when arrested, and Himrod is guaranteed to fight asthma, and suddenly Pepe's hand, which has just turned the page, freezes, and a photograph slams against his face: a six-column photo of the truck, overturned and smashed, the enormous photo of the truck, and surrounding the truck, a throng of curious onlookers, looking at the photographer, looking at Pepe looking at the onlookers, unseeing: Pepe who, blinded by tears, is facing the photo of the truck in which his father died, crushed in the spectacular crash that shook the whole neighborhood of La Teja, Montevideo, at noon on September 18, 1935.

DEATH

Not ten people went to the final recitals of the Spanish poet, Blas de Otero. But when Blas de Otero died, many thousands went to the homage held in his memory in a Madrid bullring. He had no idea.

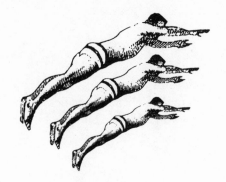

WEEPING

This happened in the jungle, in the Ecuadorian Amazon. The Shuar Indians were crying over someone's dying grandmother. They were sitting by her deathbed, crying. An observer from another world asked them:

"Why are you crying in front of her when she is still alive?"

And the ones who were weeping responded:

"So she knows how much we love her."

CELEBRATION OF LAUGHTER

José Luis Castro, the local carpenter, has a very skillful hand. The wood knows that he loves it and does not resist him.

José Luis' father had come to the River Plate from a village in Pontevedra. The son recalls his father, face lit up beneath a Panama hat, silk tie around the neck of his sky blue pajama top, and always, always telling outrageous stories. Wherever he was, the son remembers, laughter would break out. When he told stories people would come from all around to laugh and the house would be packed. At the funerals, they had to upend the coffin so everybody could fit—and thus the dead man stood up to listen with due respect to all that was being so gracefully said.

And of all the things José Luis learned from his father, the chief one was this: *"The important thing is to laugh,"* the old man taught him, *"and to laugh together."*

THE WALLS SPEAK/5

In the faculty of economic sciences in Montevideo:
Drugs produce amnesia and other things I can't remember.
In Santiago de Chile, on the banks of the Mapocho River:
Blessed are the drunkards, for they will see God twice.
In the Flores barrio of Buenos Aires:
A girlfriend without tits is more a friend than a girlfriend.

THE LAUGHTER SALESMAN

I am on the beach at Malibu, at the spot where half a century ago, the detective Philip Marlowe found one of his bodies.

Jack Miles points to a beautiful house on a rise in the distance: once the home of the man who supplied Hollywood with laughter. Ten years ago, Jack spent some time in that house before the purveyor of laughter decided to leave forever.

The house was upholstered with laughter from floor to ceiling. This man had spent his whole life collecting laughter. Tape recorder in hand, he traveled the United States, up and down, from top to bottom, in search of laughter, and he had put together the largest collection in the world. He had recorded the joy of children at play and the weary mirth of the aged. He had laughter from the north and south, east and west. On request, he could supply the laughter of celebration

or of pain or panic, the giggles of lovers, the bloodcurdling glee of ghosts, and the whooping gales and roars of lunatics, drunks and criminals. Among his many thousands of recordings, he had sincere laughter and suspect laughter, black, mulatto, and white laughter, poor, rich, and in-between.

Selling laughter to the movies, the radio, and television, he had made himself rich. But he was in truth a melancholy man and his wife could wipe the smile off anyone's lips with a single glance.

She and he left their house on the beach at Malibu, never to return. They were in flight from the Mexicans, who were coming to California in ever increasing numbers with their spicy food and the accursed habit of laughing their heads off. Now they live on the island of Tasmania, which is near Australia, but farther away.

MY RAVAGED HEAD OF HAIR

Barbers humiliate me by charging half-price.

Twenty years ago, the mirror exposed the first bare spots concealed under my mop of hair. Nowadays, I shudder with horror at the reflection of my luminous, bald pate in windows and glass storefronts.

Every hair that falls, every single strand, is a fallen comrade who before falling had a name, or at least a number.

I console myself by recalling what a compassionate friend once told me:

"If hair were important, it would grow inside our head, not outside."

I also console myself by observing that in all these years I have lost a lot of hair but not a single idea, which is cause for happiness when I compare myself to all those people living lives of regret.

CELEBRATION OF
CONTINUOUS BIRTH

Miguel Mármol served another round of Methuselah rum and told me that he was commemorating, corummerating the fiftieth anniversary of his execution. In 1932, a squadron of soldiers had finished him off, by order of the dictator Martinez.

"As far as my age goes, I am eighty-two," said Miguelito, *"but I pay no attention to that. I have many girlfriends. The doctor prescribed them."*

He told me that he was in the habit of getting up before dawn, and as soon as his eyes were open, he would sing and dance and hop around, which the neighbors below didn't like one bit.

I had gone to bring him the last volume of *Memory of Fire*. Miguel's story serves as the axis of this book: his eleven deaths and eleven resurrections over the course of his combative life. Born the first time in Ilopango, El Salvador, Miguel is the truest metaphor for Latin America. Like him, Latin America has died and been born many times. Like him, it goes on being born.

"But there's no point in talking about that," he told me. *Catholics tell me it has all been pure Providence. And the communists, my comrades, tell me it's been pure coincidence."*

I proposed that we jointly found Magical Marxism: one half reason, one half passion, and a third half mystery.

"Not a bad idea," he said.

THE DELIVERY

After three days of labor, the baby still hadn't been born.

"He's stuck. The little guy's stuck," the man said.

He had come from a remote farm in the country.

The doctor went with him.

Valise in hand, the doctor walked under the noonday sun, toward the horizon, into that desolate world where everything seems born of accursed fate. When he got there he understood.

Later, he told Gloria Galván:

"The woman was at death's door but was still panting and sweating, and her eyes were wide open. I had no experience with situations like that. I was shaking; I hadn't the faintest idea what to do. And then, as I drew back the blanket, I saw a tiny arm sticking out from between the woman's spread legs."

The doctor realized that the man had been pulling on it. The little arm was rubbed raw and lifeless: a flap of skin, black with dried blood. And the doctor thought: *There is nothing to be done.*

And yet, for whatever reason, he caressed the arm. He rubbed the inert limb with his index finger, and when he got to the hand, it suddenly closed, clutching his finger for dear life.

Then the doctor asked for boiling water and rolled up his sleeves.

RESURRECTIONS/2

It happened during the military dictatorship in Brazil.

The generals let him in so he could die in his homeland. Darcy Ribeiro returned from exile and was taken directly to the hospital in an ambulance that was waiting for him by the plane.

Darcy knew he had cancer and that it had swallowed up at least one of his lungs, but he was filled with the joy of being in the land of his birth and feeling it as alive and vibrant as ever.

Darcy's brother came from the town of Montes Claros. He came to say his last farewells. Sitting next to Darcy, he stared at his feet. He was weepy and gloomy and Darcy was doing his best to cheer him up. Thus it was that the surgeon took Darcy by the arm and led him into the hallway:

"I don't mean to discourage you," he said, *"but I think you should prepare yourself for the worst. It will be a miracle if your brother gets out of here alive."*

Darcy couldn't keep from laughing, and the doctor did not understand why.

They operated on him the next day. Darcy woke up missing a lung. With so much lung, he didn't even notice.

RESURRECTIONS/3

I was in Saint-Pierre. In what remains of Saint-Pierre.

It had been the most beautiful city in the Caribbean until a volcano burned its 30,000 inhabitants to a crisp.

The tragic prophecy of a world turned upside down: the saved were condemned and a condemned man was the only one to be saved. Three days after the catastrophe, Ludger Sylbaris, in prison for vagrancy, emerged alive, badly burned but alive: only the thick walls of the prison had been able to resist the volcano's fiery flow.

"Ladies and gentlemen! The one, the only! The man who escaped from hell! A miracle of God! Take a good look! And the squeamish should cover their eyes!"

Sylbaris became the main attraction in Barnum's circus as it traveled the world. He was a bigger draw than the bearded lady or the child with two heads. He would spread his arms and turn slowly around, displaying his raw body while the crowds shuddered with horror and pleasure.

THE THREE SIBLINGS

In Nicaragua, during the years of the war against Somoza, Sofía Montenegro slept badly.

Her brothers were the subject of her most frequent nightmares. She dreamed of an ambush and a rain of bullets in nightmares that took place in no man's land or on the path that leads to Tiscapa. After the final blast, one of Sofía's brothers, a lieutenant colonel with the dictatorship, would tear the blindfolds off the faces of his victims, and among the dead would be her other brother.

Together with that brother, the one who fell in the dream, Sofía belonged to the Sandinista Front. The enemy brother, the lieutenant colonel, had bombarded the city of Estelí and tortured prisoners. But in Sofía's dreams, the two brothers, the soldier and the *guerrillero,* had her eyes: they looked just like her; they were her.

THE TWO HEADS

Perhaps Omar Cabezas* is so named because he uses his other head. And perhaps that is how he finally reached the end of the hard road that is the Nicaraguan revolution, and that is how he has reached it alive.

Omar was a boy playing in a stone-throwing war in the city of León. Projectiles were raining down between two corners of a nondescript street when Omar saw an enormous rock heaved by the enemy coming straight at him. He saw the unmistakable trajectory of the airborne rock and began to run: he wanted to run to the other side, to escape, to save himself, but he could not keep his head from hurling itself toward its rendezvous with the rock that was its destiny, and his head arrived at the precise spot and at the precise moment to be hit and bashed in by the descending rock.

So it was that Omar lost his first head. Ever since, he has used his other head, which is not quite as crazy.

*Cabeza = head.

RESURRECTIONS/4

The liar commits a sin, says Ernesto Cardenal, because he robs words of their truth.

Back around 1524, Fray Bobadilla made a great bonfire in the village of Managua and threw the Indians' books on the flames. The books were made of deerskin with images painted in two colors: red and black.

Nicaragua had been lied to for centuries when General Sandino chose those colors, unaware that they were the colors of the ashes of the national memory.

THE ACROBAT

Luz Marina Acosta was a very small child when she discovered the Firuliche circus.

The Firuliche circus appeared one night, a magical ship of lights, from the depths of Lake Nicaragua. The cardboard trumpets of the clowns were bugles of war and the blazing rags that announced the world's greatest fiesta were lofty banners. The tent was covered with patches and so were the lions—rather superannuated lions. But the tent was a castle and the lions were kings of the jungle, and the plump lady glittering with rhinestones who bounced on the trapeze a yard above the ground was queen of the heavens.

So Luz Marina decided she would become an acrobat. And she actually jumped from some great height and in her first acrobatic feat at the age of six, broke her ribs.

Her life continued on in like fashion. In the war, the long war against the Somoza dictatorship, and in love: always soaring, always breaking her ribs.

Because once you join the Firuliche circus, you never leave.

THE FLOWERS

The Brazilian writer Nelson Rodrigues was condemned to loneliness. He had the face of a toad and the tongue of a snake and on top of his renowned ugliness and poison tongue was the notoriety of his contagious bad luck: people around him died from bullets, poverty or fatal accidents.

One day Nelson met Eleonora. On that day, the day of the discovery, when he saw her for the first time, a violent joy struck him and left him in a daze. Then he wanted to utter one of his brilliant phrases, but he grew weak in the knees and his tongue knotted up and he could only stammer little noises.

He bombarded her with flowers. He sent flowers to her apartment, on the top floor of a high building in Río de Janeiro. Each day he sent her a big bouquet of flowers, different flowers every time, never repeating a color or perfume, and he waited below. From the street, he watched Eleonora's balcony, and from the balcony, every day, she threw the flowers into the street and the cars crushed them.

This went on for fifty days. Until one day, one day at noon, the flowers Nelson had sent did not fall into the street and were not crushed by the cars.

That day at noon, he went up to the top floor, rang the bell and the door opened.

THE ANTS

Tracey Hill was a child in a Connecticut town who amused herself as befitted a child of her age, like any other tender little angel of God in the state of Connecticut or anywhere else on this planet.

One day, together with her little school companions, Tracey started throwing lighted matches into an anthill. They all enjoyed this healthy childish diversion. Tracey, however, saw something which the others didn't see or pretended not to, but which paralyzed her and remained forever engraved in her memory: faced with the dangerous fire, the ants split up into pairs and two by two, side by side, pressed close together, they waited for death.

GRANDMOTHER

Bertha Jensen's grandmother died cursing.

She had lived her whole life on tiptoe, as if apologizing for being a bother, dedicated to serving her husband and her brood of five children, she was an exemplary wife, a self-abnegating mother, a silent pillar of virtue: not a single complaint had ever passed her lips, let alone curses.

When illness struck her down, she called her husband, sat him down beside her in bed, and let loose. No one suspected that she had that drunken sailor's vocabulary. She was a long time dying. For more than a month, the grandmother vomited from her bed an unending torrent of insults and blasphemies from the depths of her being. Even her voice had changed. This woman, who had never smoked or drunk anything but milk or water, became a whiskey-voiced whore. And talking like a whore, she died, and there was general relief in the family and throughout the neighborhood.

She died where she was born, in the town of Dragor, on the coast of Denmark. Her name was Inge. She had a pretty gypsy face and liked to dress in red and sail in the sun.

GRANDFATHER

A man named Amando, born in the town of Salitre on the coast of Ecuador, presented me with the story of his grandfather.

The great grandchildren took turns looking after him. They had put a padlock and chain on the door. Don Segundo Hidalgo said that was the cause of his ailments:

"I have the rheumatism of a castrated cat."

At the age of a hundred, Don Segundo would take advantage of any carelessness to mount his horse bareback and slip out in search of girlfriends. No one knew as much about women and horses. He had populated the town of Salitre and its surroundings, since becoming a father for the first time at thirteen.

The grandfather confessed to having had three hundred women, although everyone knew he'd had over four hundred. But one of them, Blanquita, had been the womanliest woman of them all.

It had been thirty years since Blanquita died and he still invoked her name every day at dusk. Armando, the grandson who told me this story, would hide and spy upon the secret ceremony. On the balcony, illuminated by the dying light, the grandfather would open an antique powder box, a round

box with pink angels on the lid, and bring the powder puff to his nose.

"I believe I know you," he would murmur, inhaling the faint perfume of the powder, *"I believe I know you."*

And he would rock himself very gently, murmuring as he dozed off in the rocking chair.

Every evening, the grandfather would perform his homage to the woman he loved the most, and once a week he would betray her. He was unfaithful with a fat lady who prepared extremely complicated dishes on television. The grandfather, owner of the first and only television in the town of Salitre, would never miss the program. He would bathe, shower, and dress entirely in white, as if for a party, putting on his best hat, patent leather boots, a vest with golden buttons and silk necktie, and would sit right in front of the screen. While the fat lady whipped her cream and wielded her ladle, explaining the keys to some unique, exclusive, incomparable flavor, the grandfather would leer at her and blow her furtive kisses. His bank savings book poked out of the breast pocket of his suit. The grandfather placed the book that way as if carelessly, so the fat lady would see he was no poor ragamuffin.

FUGA, THE FAST ONE

Maité Piñero, who had just arrived from El Salvador, brought me the news:

"He's dead."

An enemy plane was quicker than he was. After the attack, his compañeros buried him. They buried him at nightfall. Everyone looked away. They could not face each other.

Fuga had arrived three or four years earlier and had come to stay. He arrived with the dawn in the days of heavy rain and installed himself in the middle of the camp under the rain. The rain pounded him but he stayed put.

And he stayed put when the downpour ended: a donkey, or the statue of a donkey beaten and tattered, whose one eye stared impassively out of his face for all time.

The guerrillas threw him out. They insulted him, kicked him, shoved him; he paid no attention.

So he stayed. They called him Fuga because he was the quickest to escape in the turmoil of the bombings. They sent him away on difficult fetch-and-carry missions but he always returned. The boys were constantly on the move, crossing the charred mountains of San Miguel from one side to another, and he always found them. And when the army had them surrounded, Fuga found them a way through the minefields as though it were a piece of cake, and with his saddlebags stuffed with coffee, tortillas, cigarettes and bullets, he would penetrate enemy lines as though it were nothing.

"Don't betray us, Fuga," they asked him. And he would gaze at them unblinking with his one eye.

The little donkey knew everything. He knew the bases of operation and the stashes of weapons and provisions, the paths and shortcuts, the crossing chosen for the next ambush, and he also knew the friends of the guerrillas in every village. And Fuga knew more, much more, everything there was to know: he was the safeguard of confidences. Because the little donkey knew how to listen to everyone's sorrows and doubts and deepest secrets, and even the most macho of machos, silent men of iron, allowed themselves to weep in his presence.

CELEBRATION OF FRIENDSHIP/1

On the outskirts of Havana, they call friends *mi tierra,* my country, or *mi sangre,* my blood.

In Caracas, a friend is *mi pana,* my bread, or *mi llave,* my key: *pana* from *panadería,* bakery, the source of wholesome bread to sate the hunger of the soul; *llave,* from . . .

"Key, from key," Mario Benedetti tells me.

And he tells how, when he lived in Buenos Aires in times of terror, he would carry five alternate keys on his key ring: the keys to five houses, to five friends: the keys that proved his salvation.

CELEBRATION OF FRIENDSHIP/2

Juan Gelman told me how, on an avenue in Paris, a woman beat off an entire battalion of municipal workers with her umbrella. The workers were catching pigeons when she sallied forth from an incredible Model T, one of those museum pieces with a crank-starter, and brandishing her umbrella, launched her attack.

Wielding her sword with both hands, she pressed forward, her righteous umbrella smashing the nets they were using to snare pigeons. Then, as the pigeons fled in a tumult of white, the woman turned her umbrella on the workers.

The workers shielded themselves with their arms as best they could, stammering protests which she ignored: Show some respect, ma'am, if you please, we're trying to work, we're just following orders, ma'am, why don't you go take a whack at the mayor, calm down, ma'am, what's eating you, this lady has gone mad. . . .

When the furious woman's arm grew tired and she leaned against a wall to catch her breath, the workers demanded an explanation.

After a long silence, she said:

"My son died."

The workers told her they were very sorry, but that they were not to blame. They also said that they had a lot to do that morning, you understand. . . .

"My son died," she said again.

And the workers: yes, yes, but they had to earn a living, that there were millions of pigeons flying loose throughout Paris, that those bloody pigeons were the plague of the city—

"Cretins!" the woman exploded.

And to the confusion of the workers, she said:

"My son died and became a pigeon."

The workers fell silent, and stood in thought for quite a while. Finally, pointing to the pigeons that populated the skies, the tile roofs, and the sidewalks, they proposed to her:

"Ma'am: Why don't you take your son and let us work in peace?"

She adjusted her black hat:

"Oh no! Absolutely not!"

She looked through the workers as if they were made of glass, and said with great serenity:

"I don't know which of the pigeons is my son. And even if I did know, I wouldn't take him away. For what right have I to separate him from his friends?"

GELMAN

The poet Juan Gelman writes, hoisting himself from the rubble of his life, from its dust and debris.

The Argentine military, whose atrocities would have given Hitler an incurable inferiority complex, hit him where it hurt the most. In 1976, they kidnapped his children. They took the children instead of him. They tortured his daughter, Nora, and let her go. They murdered and disappeared his son, Marcelo, together with his pregnant compañera.

Instead of him: they took his children because he was not at home. How does one survive such a tragedy? That is: survive without one's soul being extinguished? I've often wondered these last years. I've often imagined that horrible feeling of having one's life usurped, the nightmare of the father who imagines he has stolen from his son the air he breathes, the father who wakes in the middle of the night, bathed in sweat: *"I didn't kill you, I didn't kill you."* And I've wondered: if God exists, why does he just walk on by? Could God be an atheist?

ART AND TIME

"Who are my contemporaries?" Juan Gelman asks himself.

Juan says that sometimes he comes across men who smell of fear, in Buenos Aires, Paris, or anywhere in the world, and feels that these men are not his contemporaries. But there is a Chinese who, thousands of years ago, wrote a poem about a goatherd who is far from his beloved, and yet can hear in the middle of the night, in the middle of the snow, the sound of her comb running through her hair. And reading this distant poem, Juan finds that yes, these people—the poet, the goatherd and the woman—are truly his contemporaries.

A PROFESSION OF FAITH

Yes, indeed: however hurt and shattered one might be, one can always find contemporaries anywhere in time, and compatriots anywhere in space. And wherever this happens, and for as long as it lasts, one is lucky to feel one is something in the infinite loneliness of the universe: something more than a ridiculous speck of dust, more than just a fleeting moment.

CORTÁZAR

With just one arm, he embraced both of us. His arm was very long, as before, but the rest of him was quite reduced, for which reason Helena dreamed him with suspicion, not sure whether to believe it or not. Julio Cortázar explained that he had recovered thanks to a Japanese machine, a very good machine but still in the experimental stage, and that by mistake the machine had turned him into a dwarf.

Julio told us that the emotions of the living come to the dead as letters, and that he had wanted to come back to life because of the great pain he felt for the pain his death had caused us. Furthermore, he said, being dead is rather boring. Julio said he wanted very much to write a story about that.

CHRONICLE OF THE CITY
OF MONTEVIDEO

Julio César Puppo, known as The Lumberjack, and Alfred Gravina met one night in a café in the neighborhood of Villa Dolores. And so, by chance, they discovered they were neighbors.

"So close without knowing it."

They offered each other a drink, then another.

"You look very well."

"Don't you believe it."

And they spent several hours and plenty of drinks speaking of the crazy weather and the cost of living, of lost friends and the places that no longer existed, of memories from their early youth:

"Remember?"

"Of course I remember."

When the café finally closed its doors, Gravina accompanied The Lumberjack to the door of his house. But then The Lumberjack wanted to reciprocate:

"I'll come with you."

"Don't bother."

"It's no problem."

And they spent the whole night going back and forth. Sometimes they would be stopped by some sudden memory or the need for a little more stability, but then they would immediately continue going from one corner to the other, from the house of one to the house of the other, from one door to the other, as if drawn and propelled by an invisible pendulum, loving each other without saying so and embracing without touching.

THE BARBED WIRE FENCE

The order to line up came with violent suddenness. It was the coldest night of that year and of many years and a hostile fog enveloped everything.

With yells and gun butts, the prisoners were lined up facing the barbed wire fence that surrounded the barracks. From the towers, searchlights pierced the fog and slowly played along the long file of gray uniforms, frozen hands and shaven heads.

Turning around was prohibited. The prisoners heard the sound of boots running and the metallic click of machine guns being readied for firing. Then, silence.

In those days a rumor had run through the prison:

"They're going to kill us all."

Mario Dufort was one of those prisoners and he was sweating ice. Like everyone else, his arms were spread and his hands clutched the barbed wire: he was trembling and the barbed wire was trembling. He said to himself, *trembling from the cold,* and then repeated it. He didn't believe it.

He was ashamed of his fear. He felt exposed by the spectacle he was giving his comrades. And he let go of the wire.

But the wire kept on trembling. Shaken by all the others, the wire went on trembling.

And then Mario understood.

HEAVEN AND HELL

I arrived in Bluefields, on the Nicaraguan coast, the day after an attack by the Contras. There were many dead and wounded. I was in the hospital when one of the survivors of the skirmish, a young boy, awoke from anesthesia. He woke up without arms, looked at the doctor, and said:

"*Kill me.*"

I felt a knot in my stomach.

That night, an atrocious night, the air was boiling. I threw myself down on a terrace, alone, face to the sky. Not far from there, music rang out loudly. In spite of it all, the people of Bluefields were celebrating the traditional fiesta of the May-pole. The people were dancing jubilantly around the ceremonial tree. But I, stretched out on the terrace, didn't want to hear the music, or anything at all, and I was trying not to feel, not to remember, not to think about anything, anything whatsoever. And there I was, swatting away at sounds, sadness and mosquitos, my eyes fixed on the night sky, when a child of Bluefields whom I didn't know lay down beside me and began looking at the sky as I was, in silence.

Then a shooting star fell. I could have made a wish but it didn't occur to me.

And the child explained:

"*You know why stars fall? It's God's fault. God sticks them up badly. He sticks the stars on with rice water.*"

I greeted the dawn dancing.

CHRONICLE OF THE CITY OF MANAGUA

I was invited to dinner by Comandante Tomás Borge. I hadn't met him before. He had the reputation of being the toughest of them all, the one people feared the most. There were other guests at the table, wonderful people. He said nothing, or next to nothing. He was watching me, sizing me up.

The second time, we had dinner alone. Tomás was more open, freely answering my questions about the old days when they were founding the Sandinista Front. And around midnight, like someone who is avoiding saying what he actually means, he said:

"All right now, tell me a movie."

I pleaded with him, explaining that I lived in Calella, a small town where few movies were shown, old movies . . .

"Tell me one," he insisted, ordered. *"Any movie—any one, even if it isn't new."*

So I told him a comedy. I told it. I acted it out. I tried to summarize but he demanded details. And as soon as I finished:

"Another one."

I told him a gangster film with a lousy ending.

"Another."

I told him a western.

"Another."

I told him a love story, making it up out of whole cloth.

I think dawn was breaking when, pleading for mercy, I gave up and went off to bed.

I met him a week later. Tomás apologized:

"I squeezed the last drop out of you the other night. It's just that I like the movies so much, I'm crazy about them. And I can never go."

I told him that it was perfectly understandable. He was Nicaragua's minister of the interior in the middle of a war. The enemy was giving no quarter and there was no time for the movies or other such luxuries.

"No, no," he corrected me. *"Time I've got. Time. . . . You can make time if you want to. It's not for lack of time. In the past, when I was living underground, incognito, I arranged to go to the movies. But now . . ."*

I didn't ask. He paused and then went on:

"I can't go to the movies because . . . because when I'm at the movies, I cry."

"Ah," I said. *"Me too."*

"Of course," he said. *"I knew it right away. As soon as I saw you, I thought: 'This guy cries at the movies.' "*

THE CHALLENGE

"They didn't succeed in turning us into them," Cacho El Kadri wrote to me.

It was in the last days of the military dictatorship in Uruguay. We had eaten fear for breakfast, fear for lunch and for dinner, fear. But they had not succeeded in turning us into them.

Gabriel Caro, a Colombian who fought in Nicaragua, tells me that a Swiss fell by his side, ripped apart by the blast of a machine gun, and no one knew his name. This happened on the southern front, a few nights north of the San Juan River, shortly before the defeat of the Somoza dictatorship. No one knew his name, no one knew anything about that silent blond militiaman who had gone so far as to die for Nicaragua, for the Revolution, for the moon. The Swiss fell, shouting something that nobody understood. He fell yelling:

"Long live Bakunin!"

And as I listen to Gabriel telling the story of the Swiss, my memory lights up.

Years ago, in Montevideo, Carlos Bonavita spoke to me of an uncle or great uncle of his, who wrote war dispatches at the time of the Gaucho wars on the Uruguayan plains. This uncle or great uncle was counting the dead on the bank of the river where a battle—I don't know which—had occurred. By the color of their headbands he could tell which side they were on. And while engaged in this, he turned over a corpse and froze. The soldier was very young, an angel with sad eyes. Over his black hair, red with blood, the white hairband said: *For the Fatherland and for her.* The bullet had pierced the word "her."

CELEBRATION OF COURAGE/2

I asked him if he had seen an execution by firing squad. Yes, he had seen one.

El Chino Heras had seen a colonel shot at the end of 1960, in the La Cabaña barracks. Many executioners had served the Batista dictatorship, ugly beasts at the service of pain and death. That colonel had been one of the worst, one of the most.

I was with a group of friends in a hotel room in Havana. El Chino related how the colonel had not wanted them to blindfold him and his last request had not been for a cigarette: the colonel asked that they let him direct his own execution.

The colonel shouted *"Ready!"* Then: *"Aim!"* As he was about to shout *"Fire!"* the bolt of one soldier's gun jammed. Then the colonel interrupted the ceremony. *"Keep calm,"* he said before the double row of men who were to kill him. They were so close he could almost touch them:

"Keep calm," he said. *"Don't get nervous."*

And again he ordered them to ready their guns and aim.

And when all was ready again, he ordered them to fire. And he fell.

El Chino told of the death of the colonel and no one said a word. There were several of us in the room and we were all silent.

Stretched out like a cat on the bed was a girl dressed in red. I don't recall her name. I recall her legs. She didn't say anything either.

Two or three bottles of rum made the rounds and finally everyone went off to bed. She went too. Before leaving, she looked at El Chino from the half-opened door, smiled at him and said:

"Thank you, I didn't know the details. Thanks for telling me."

Later we found out that the colonel was her father.

A dignified death always makes a good story, even when it is the dignified death of a sonofabitch. I wanted to write about it but couldn't. Time passed and I forgot it.

Of the girl, I never heard another word.

Sergio Vuskovic tells me of the last days of José Tohá.

"He committed suicide," said General Pinochet.

"The government cannot guarantee the immortality of anyone," wrote a journalist in the official press.

"He was weak on account of his nerves," said General Leigh.

The Chilean generals hated him. Tohá had been Minister of Defense in the Allende government and knew their secrets.

They were holding him in a concentration camp on Dawson Island, to the south of the south.

The prisoners were sentenced to forced labor. Under the rain, in the mud or snow, the prisoners hauled stones, built walls, laid drains, drove posts and hung barbed wire.

Tohá, who was over six feet tall, weighed one hundred and ten pounds. He would faint under questioning. They questioned him tied to a chair, blindfolded. When he came to, he wouldn't have the strength to speak, yet would whisper:

"Listen, officer."

He would whisper:

"Long live the poor people of the world."

After lying prostrate in the barracks for some time, one day he got to his feet. It was the last day he would stand up.

It was extremely cold as always, but the sun was shining. Someone got him a nice hot cup of coffee and Jorquera the black man whistled a Gardel tango for him—one of those old tangos he loved so well.

His legs trembled and his knees gave way with every step, but Tohá danced that tango. He danced it with a broom, one as gaunt as the other, Tohá pressing the handle of the broom against his patrician face, his eyes shut tight with emotion, until at one turn, he fell broken to the ground and couldn't get up.

He was never seen again.

CELEBRATION OF COURAGE/4

The petty Right and the puritan Left have devoted a large measure of their zeal to discussing whether Salvador Allende committed suicide or not.

Allende had announced that he would not leave the presidential palace alive. It is a tradition in Latin America: they all say it. Later, when the coup d'état occurs, they are on the first plane out.

After many hours of bombing and shooting, Allende was still fighting amidst the rubble. Then he called over his closest collaborators, who were resisting alongside him, and told them:

"You go down. I'll be there in a minute."

They believed him and left, and Allende remained alone in the burning palace.

What does it matter whose finger it was that fired the final shot?

A SECRET MUSCLE

One memorable noon, one noon of my exile, I was writing, reading or getting bored in my house on the Barcelona coast, when the phone rang and brought me, to my surprise, the voice of Fico.

Fico had been in jail for more than two years. He had been set free the previous day. The plane had brought him from the cell in Buenos Aires to the airport in London. He was calling me from that airport to ask if I would go there: Come on the first plane, I have lots to tell you, there's so much to talk about. But there's one thing I want to tell you right now. I want you to know:

"I'm not sorry for anything."

And that same evening, we met in London.

The next day, I went with him to the dentist. There was nothing to be done. The electric shocks in the torture chambers had loosened his upper teeth, and they had to be given up for lost.

Fico Vogelius was the businessman who had financed the magazine *Crisis,* and he had put not only money but his soul and life into that venture and had given me the freedom to do whatever I wanted with the magazine. While it lasted—three years, forty issues—*Crisis* managed to be a stubborn act of faith in the creative and solitary word, the word that is not,

nor tries to be, neutral, the human voice that is not an echo or empty sound.

For that crime, for the unforgivable crime of *Crisis,* the Argentine military dictatorship had kidnapped Fico, jailed him and tortured him. He had saved his life by a hair, by managing to yell out his name as he was being kidnapped.

The magazine had fallen without bending and we were proud of that. Fico had a bottle of God-knows-what old and dear French wine. With that wine, in London, we drank to the health of the past, still a compañero worthy of confidence.

Later, some years later, the military dictatorship came to an end. And in 1985 Fico decided that *Crisis* should be revived. And he was engaged in that, again disposed to burn time and money, when he learned that he had cancer.

He consulted various doctors in various countries. Some gave him until October to live, others until November. Not beyond November was the sentence. He walked around like a corpse, collapsing from one operation to another, but a defiant light shone in his eyes.

Crisis reappeared in April of 1986. The day following its rebirth, half a year beyond all prognostications, Fico allowed himself to die.

ANOTHER SECRET MUSCLE

During her final years, my grandmother didn't get along well at all with her body. Her body, the body of an exhausted spider, declined to obey her.

"It's a good thing your mind gets a free ride," she said.

I was far away, in exile. In Montevideo my grandmother felt that her hour had arrived. Before dying, she wanted to visit my house, body and all.

She arrived by plane, accompanied by my Aunt Emma. She had traveled through clouds, through waves, convinced that she was on a ship. And when the plane flew through a storm, she thought she was in a carriage, bouncing over a cobbled street.

She stayed with us for a month. She ate baby's pap and stole candies. She would wake up in the middle of the night, wanting to play chess or fighting with my grandfather who had died forty years back. Sometimes she would try to escape onto the beach but her legs would get all tangled up before she reached the stairs.

Finally she said:

"Now I can die."

She said she wasn't going to die in Spain. She wanted to spare me all the bureaucratic tangles, the transfer of her body and all that: she said she well knew how much I hated all that red tape.

And she returned to Montevideo. She visited the whole family, house by house, relative by relative, so that all might see she had returned in the best of shape and that the trip was not to be blamed. Then, a week after her arrival, she lay down and died.

Her sons scattered her ashes beneath the tree she had chosen.

Sometimes, Granny comes to see me in dreams. I am walking by a river and she is a fish accompanying me, gliding softly, softly through the water.

THE FIESTA

The sun was gentle, the air clear, and the sky cloudless.

Buried in the sand, the clay pot steamed. As they went from ocean to mouth, the shrimp passed through the hands of Fernando, master of ceremonies, who bathed them in a holy water of salt, onions, and garlic. There was good wine. Seated in a circle, we friends shared the wine and shrimp and the ocean that spread out free and luminous at our feet.

As it took place, that happiness was already being remembered by our memory. It would never end, nor would we. For we are all mortal until the first kiss and the second glass, which is something everyone knows, no matter how small his or her knowledge.

FINGERPRINTS

I was born and raised under the stars of the Southern Cross.

Wherever I go, they follow me. Under the sparkling Southern Cross, I live out the stages of my fate.

I have no god. If I had one, I would beseech him not to let me meet death, not yet. I still have a long way to go. There are moons at which I have not yet howled and suns which have not yet set me alight. I have still not swum in all the seas of the world, of which they say there are seven, nor in all the rivers of Paradise, of which they say there are four.

In Montevideo, a child explains:

"I never want to die, because I want to play forever."

270   *EDUARDO GALEANO*

THE AIR AND THE WIND

Like San Fernando's little ass, I travel the roads partly on foot, just walking.

Sometimes I recognize myself in others. I recognize myself in those who will endure, friends who will shelter me, beautiful holy fools of justice and flying creatures of beauty and other bums and vagrants who walk the earth and will continue walking, just as the stars will continue in the night and the waves in the sea. Then, when I recognize myself in them, I am the air, coming to know myself as part of the wind.

I think it was Vallejo, César Vallejo, who said that sometimes the wind changes its air.

When I am no longer, the wind will be, will continue being.

THE GUST

The wind whistles within me.

I am naked. Master of nothing, master of no one, not even master of my own convictions, I am my face in the wind, against the wind, and I am the wind that strikes my face.

Index